D1060845

# dianastyle

# dianastyle

Colin McDowell

Foreword by

MANOLO BLAHNIK

ST. MARTIN'S PRESS
NEW YORK

DIANA STYLE.


For information, address St. Martin's Press, 175 Fifth Avenue, New York, N.Y. 10010.

www.stmartins.com

Design by Isobel Gillan
Picture research by Nadine Bazar

ISBN-13: 978-0-312-37537-9
ISBN-10: 0-312-37537-9

First published in Great Britain by Aurum Press Ltd.

First U.S. Edition: August 2007

10 9 8 7 6 5 4 3 2 1

# contents

# foreword
# by Manolo Blahnik

IMAGES OF A PARTICULAR PERIOD tend to date quickly. They may capture the era's spirit to perfection, but once it's over, they become instantly anachronistic. It is the clothes, the hair or simply the texture of the photograph itself that freezes the sitter forever into a particular moment in time, making it instantly recognizable.

When one looks at images of the late Princess of Wales, there is something in them that transcends the period in which they were taken – which is an irony, since she became so symbolic of her time. Of course, there are the dresses, and sometimes not-so-graceful hats, or hairstyles that will make it possible for those who care about such matters to identify the exact date and location, but there was more to this magnificent woman than that.

My first memory of her is as a young lady, in January 1980, some time before her engagement to the Prince of Wales. She was in Old Church Street, having just bought a pair of shoes at our shop. I can still see her placing the bag into the pannier of her bicycle. And I remember those eyes, those eyes already then arresting: sometimes downcast, curious, but full of wonder and mischievousness. Often, you couldn't tell what was going on behind them, but you were instantly captivated and entrapped.

Over the years, it was joyous to watch her flourish. As she searched for her own style, she sometimes made mistakes, which were immediately forgiven because they were made with such sincerity and because we knew that she was simply trying to find a look that finally belonged to her. But that didn't stop the critics – always ready to leap at the first opportunity – from attacking her for the most banal of the so-called style faux pas.

Yet in spite of the fashion errors, she became one of the most influential women of the twentieth century. Millions in her native England and around the world tried unsuccessfully to capture her look, mostly failing not because they couldn't get hold of the clothes, or the jewels, but because what she had was not just about clothes, or make-up, or hair, but something much deeper, an elusive quality that most refer to as grace or elegance – qualities with which she was born and which now seem almost too trivial to attribute to someone so wonderful. And yet again, those eyes!

It is a peculiar combination that made Diana, Princess of Wales as iconic as she eventually became. It was not only the right dresses or the allure, which – as time eventually taught us – turned out to be minor players in the story of her life. It was also her particular type of humility, a heart as big as the world and a sweetness of character that was part of the phenomenon, that helped turn the Princess of Wales into an icon forever worthy of her stature.

It was a privilege and an honour for me to serve her.

‘Black to me was the smartest colour you could possibly have at the age of nineteen. It was a real grown-up dress.’

DIANA, PRINCESS OF WALES

# introduction
# a tale of two dresses

IT WAS ONE OF DIANA’S MOST difficult days. In the thirteen years since her engagement to Prince Charles, she had become the most photographed woman in the world. She was a fashion icon around the globe, almost as famous for her wardrobe, her blonde hair and her lean frame as for her charity work, her efforts to increase the profile of AIDS sufferers, and her role as the mother of the future king. No woman has ever been more photographed. Day after day, she knew she must look immaculate; it came with the job.

But that part of Diana’s life was passing. Not for the first time, she was going through an epochal upheaval. On 29 June 1994, she wanted to mark the occasion, and she chose the way she knew best: her appearance. Diana had learned a thing or two about how to present herself, and photographers such as Tim Graham colluded with her to keep her image fresh. On this special night, she thought particularly carefully about the image she wanted to achieve.

The British broadcaster Jonathan Dimbleby had made a documentary about Prince Charles, with the prince’s involvement, that was scheduled to be aired on the BBC that evening. It was the latest instalment in the soap opera of the royal marriage, or what the tabloids dubbed the ‘War of the Windsors’. Charles would confide to his friend Jonathan Dimbleby that he had been unfaithful to Diana with his long-time lover Camilla Parker-Bowles. It was a final confirmation that the marriage was a sham. Divorce was inevitable. But

Diana did not want anyone to feel sorry for her. She couldn't do what other women might do in the same situation – find solace in her friends and a few glasses of wine – but she could do far better.

That evening she was due to attend a fund-raising dinner hosted by *Vanity Fair* at the Serpentine Gallery, of which she was the patron. She had originally planned to wear a dress designed by Valentino, but his fashion house had released a premature and unauthorized press statement announcing details of the dress, much to Diana's displeasure. That was a breach of royal protocol about which she complained to her closest fashion adviser, Anna Harvey of British *Vogue*, who was equally unhappy at this display of crude opportunism. Instead, Diana and her butler Paul Burrell selected an alternative outfit. A couple of years earlier, Diana had purchased a capped-sleeve, asymmetrically ruched black dress by Christina Stambolian. It was the only one the princess ever bought from the Athens-trained designer and it would have more impact than almost any other outfit Diana had ever worn.

Diana's choice of black was itself highly significant. It was the first time she had appeared in the colour at an official engagement other than a funeral since before her wedding in 1981. On that occasion, she had worn a long black gown designed by David and Elizabeth Emanuel for her first official appearance as the Prince of Wales's fiancée. She had selected it off the peg and the designers had no time to fit it precisely for her, so that the low-cut neckline made Diana's cleavage a little too prominent. With her 18-carat sapphire in a fourteen-diamond ring on her finger and the $1000 strapless gown on her back, Diana stepped out of the car to what the BBC described as 'audible gasps'.

Worn by the fiancée of virtually anyone else in the country, the dress would have caused little reaction beyond the odd admiring glance. On the future wife of the Prince of Wales, it created a storm. Journalists and photographers were beside themselves with excitement. Not only was the heir to the throne finally about to be married, but their first impressions of Diana as a demure, slightly chubby Sloane Ranger had turned out to be not entirely accurate. Here was a hint that she had a more daring side.

The press were not the only ones to get excited by the dress. Royal insiders knew that the royal family, including the Queen, would be livid. Not only was this the first evidence of Diana's potential to steal the Windsor show, but also, and more importantly, it was a breach of protocol. For centuries, the royals had worn black only for funerals and for mourning. There are many different accounts of exactly who said what to whom. In *Diana: Her True Story*, Andrew Morton reports that Prince Charles told Diana when she appeared in his study to show off the dress that only people in mourning wore black. Other accounts suggest the Queen let it be known that she never wanted to see Diana in a similar dress again.

Diana's excuse was simple. She later recalled, 'Black to me was the smartest colour you could possibly have at the age of nineteen. It was a real grown-up dress'. And of course she was right. For generations of women, black had been a sophisticated, glamorous colour with the advantages of being slimming and sleek. In the Twenties, Coco Chanel had made the little black dress de rigueur as part of the wardrobe of all fashionable women. In the Eighties, Donna Karan and others designers had established black as part of the work uniform for serious women, just as it long had been for their male counterparts.

Diana felt that being a princess, too, was serious work: it was her job to make an appearance. But on that very first outing, inexperience led her into error. Whether she had underestimated the strict protocol of the royal family or not realized that camera lenses would be pointing at her from all angles – including, in this case, straight at her décolleté – Diana's first foray into official dressing occasioned more negative comment than positive.

Jump forward again thirteen years, as Lord Palumbo steps forward to welcome Diana to the dinner at the Serpentine Gallery in London's Hyde Park on the night of Prince Charles's TV documentary appearance. The princess seems taller; certainly slimmer. Her bust is emphasized but safely concealed. Her legs – hailed by most designers as her best feature – are long and shapely, accentuated by the ruched skirt, which is caught up in a sash that falls at the princess's side. Her bare shoulders are broad; her arm muscles have a hint of definition from hours of work in the gym and the swimming pool. Her hair is more controlled, revealing more of her face, and her slender neck is highlighted by a multi-stranded pearl choker. She gets out of the limousine in a practised way that avoids awkward movements or revealing glimpses of her décolletage or thighs. While she shakes Lord Palumbo's hand, her small black clasp bag fits comfortably in her free hand.

This is a picture of a woman in control. This is a woman who can no longer be taken by surprise by the media. She knows the cameras will be there, and

she knows how to give them what they want – and get what she wants in return. The next day, she sees that her stratagem has worked: her stunning appearance dominates the front pages of the popular press, making her husband's revelations take second place. Not for the first time, Diana has upstaged the heir to the throne and the family often referred to, with comic mafia overtones, as the Firm. Not for the first time, she had used the simplest of means – her physical appearance – to send a message to millions of members of the public: I'm doing fine by myself. As fashion messages go, few could be stronger. In the *Telegraph Magazine* the dress was hailed as 'the brave, wicked, historic little "Serpentine Cocktail"'. It said that the 'devastating wisp of black chiffon' was 'possibly the most strategic dress ever worn by a woman in modern times'.

THIS BOOK IS THE STORY of the journey between those two black dresses and beyond – to the last phase of Diana's life, when she could finally define her own style without any regard for an official position. It is concerned not with the details of Diana's life, by turns fascinating and tragic; that story has been told often enough and is by now known by virtually everyone. Rather, *Diana Style* traces the evolution of an appearance and what it revealed about her life story. It also examines Diana's interactions with the individuals who made it possible, from the designers themselves to the dressers and advisers, the press and the public they serve, to whom her fashion message was ultimately directed. The clothes, the changes in body shape and the constantly perfect hair – they all played their roles in making Diana what she herself called 'the Queen of people's hearts'. By the time of her death, Diana had evolved from the naive teenager with no concept of personal style into an acknowledged fashion leader and one of the most stylish women on the planet. The story of two contrasting black dresses illustrates clearly how far Diana had come.

It was exciting.

**That lady was**

There aren't any truly

truly glamorous.

glamorous people today…

MURRAY ARBEID

> 'It was one of the things I always noticed about [Diana] before we got married. She had a very good sense of style and design.'
>
> PRINCE CHARLES

# country **casual**

ACCORDING TO ONE'S POINT OF VIEW, the marriage of Prince Charles and Lady Diana Spencer on 29 July 1981 was the wedding of the year, of the decade, or even of the century. It gripped the attention not just of the British, who were given a day off work to celebrate, but of much of the rest of the world. It was a spectacle worthy of the moment: the bride stepped from her carriage at St Paul's Cathedral dressed like a fairytale princess in ivory silk and lace, followed by the longest train in the history of royal brides, at a length of twenty-five feet.

Much of the day followed royal protocol. If not precisely rules, there were certainly traditions about who should be invited, suitable venues, even which members of the royal family shared which coaches, and the order of their procession through the crowds that had been gathering along the route since the early hours. After the service, again, the return journey meticulously observed precedent, right up to the appearance by the whole family on the balcony at Buckingham Palace and the famous public kiss between the new husband and wife.

The British royal family had been staging such formal pomp-and-circumstance occasions for centuries, using them as a way to excite and satisfy its subjects with a display of grandeur that invited popular participation and yet managed to keep the public at arm's length from its rulers. As the

nineteenth-century historian Walter Bagehot pointed out, nothing must be allowed to let daylight in upon magic. Weddings, funerals, coronations, investitures, jubilees: these were occasions at which the British royal family was greatly experienced and greatly skilled. So, magic it was.

But in the midst of all the day's regulated ceremony came a single moment, Diana's emergence from her carriage into her new life, that was not part of the official script. India Hicks, one of the young bridesmaids, noted, 'I have seen crowds and listened to applause and things, but I have never heard anything like that noise when Diana got out of the carriage. It was absolutely extraordinary – the cheers and cries of the people'. This heart-stopping moment in the middle of the day was the creation of three young people with no experience of royalty or its traditions: two young fashion designers who had barely graduated from the Royal College of Art and a nineteen-year-old member of one of the less well-known of Britain's aristocratic families, Lady Diana Spencer.

The vision created when the bride stepped out of the glass carriage in a billowing sea of ivory silk and lace was pure romance. We were all invited into a child's picture of what a princess should look like in the modern world: a princess from the past, from the days of Marie Antoinette, or from the movies, from *Cinderella* or *Snow White*. This was a vision of royalty that owed more to Hollywood and Walt Disney than it did to late twentieth-century Britain or emerging Eighties' attitudes.

How fragile that vision was, how little it took account of the practicalities of marrying into a royal family struggling to preserve its own role in a changing world, should have been clear for all to see. It is a testament to the strength of the innocent vision of those three young people, and to the way in which it appealed to the yearnings of millions of ordinary citizens, that virtually everyone chose for many years to ignore the fact. It was only when there was clear and unequivocal evidence that the dream had turned into a nightmare that reality struck back. Even so, the fairytale persists: at the Spencers' ancestral home at Althorp, visitors still queue up to marvel at Diana's wedding dress, on display without apparent irony only yards from the isolated island on which it is assumed her remains lie in an unmarked grave, buried beneath concrete for security.

All of this, of course, lay in the future on the day that Lady Diana Spencer married into the royal family. For the moment, it seemed clear that the whole world shared the excitement of the young woman stepping out of the carriage. It was a romance straight out of the pages of a Barbara Cartland novel. But even Cartland, Diana's stepmother's own mother, could not have concocted this potent tale of romantic love in which a shy, gawky, mousey teenager had captured her own handsome prince. It was perhaps saying something for the spirit of the occasion that Charles did indeed seem like a handsome prince. Long touted as the nation's most eligible bachelor, perhaps as *the* world's most eligible bachelor, Charles's desirability owed very much more to his social position and future prospects than it did to his Windsor looks.

A SUCCESSION OF ROYAL GIRLFRIENDS had been paraded in the tabloid press, which, at the end of the 1970s, was beginning to earn a reputation for sensational, intrusive journalism about gossip and celebrity. Without that change of tone in the popular newspapers, the saga of the Windsors' search for the mother of an heir to the throne may well have remained a minor concern for most people. As it was, Charles's choice of girlfriends became a matter of intense public speculation. (There were few clues in his admission of his deep appreciation of Barbra Streisand and the Three Degrees.) Every new candidate from among Britain's leading families soon disappeared, however, including Sarah Spencer, with whom he began a relationship in June 1977 that fizzled out after a year or so.

It was at this time, in the middle of a ploughed field during a November shooting party near Althorp, that Charles was introduced to Sarah's sixteen-year-old sister Diana, a rather bored bystander wearing a borrowed anorak, corduroy trousers and Wellington boots. Diana later recalled that the Spencers held a dance in honour of the prince's visit. She recalled, 'I stayed out of the way. I remember being a fat, podgy, no make-up, unsmart lady, but I made a lot of noise and he liked that'. Diana, like her sister, addressed Prince Charles as 'Sir'. It was only years later, after their official engagement, that she was allowed to address him as Charles. Already it must have been clear, even to a child described by her parents as being young for her age, that no relationship with such a man could in any way be seen as ordinary.

Walter Bagehot's words, written more than one hundred years earlier, sum up the enviable role to which Charles had been born as the eldest son of the monarch. With the Prince Regent, later George IV, in mind, he wrote:

'All the world and all the glory of it, whatever is most attractive, whatever is most seductive, has always been offered to the Prince of Wales of the day, and always will be'. He went on to offer a vision that proved prophetic: 'It is not rational to expect the best virtue where temptation is applied in the most trying form at the frailest time of human life'. Prince Charles is alleged to have expressed the same sentiments to his wife in a far more direct fashion: 'Do you really expect me to be the first Prince of Wales in history not to have a mistress?'

For Charles, it was clear: producing an heir to the throne was official business, and it was worth waiting to recruit the right candidate to be the mother of this heir. He was guided in his choice by his close friend Camilla Parker-Bowles, who, along with his beloved grandmother, the Queen Mother, became the unofficial arbiter of his prospective partners. After the end of his relationship with Sarah Spencer, Charles's name was linked closely with both Lady Amanda Knatchbull, granddaughter of the recently assassinated Earl Mountbatten, and with Anna Wallace, the Scottish landowner's daughter.

Then, sitting on hay bales at a house party after a polo match in July 1980, Charles again met the youngest Spencer daughter. Diana expressed her sympathy about the loss of Lord Mountbatten, at whose funeral she had seen Charles on TV. She said, 'It's wrong, you're lonely, you should be with somebody to look after you'. That was the conversation that began it all. He was nearly thirty-three; she was nineteen. He had a world-weary, pragmatic view of the business of royalty; she wanted to nurture and look after the man trapped on his own at the heart of royal ceremony. But ultimately they were from different worlds.

THERE WAS NOTHING IN DIANA'S HERITAGE and upbringing that had prepared her either for entering this different world or for the task of becoming a princess – the sharp-tongued might say that she was unprepared for any task. Unlike most people, however, she was at least familiar with the Queen's children and with the upper echelons of British society. She may have been the first British commoner to marry into the royal family for more than 300 years, but there was nothing ordinary about her social status or about the privilege the Spencers enjoyed. They could trace their ancestry back to the Stuart kings of the seventeenth century, even allegedly, if a little less

convincingly, back to William the Conqueror. Indeed, there were few commentators who, after the engagement had been announced, could resist the temptation to point out that the Spencers' genealogy was in almost every way superior to that of the Windsors themselves.

Being a Spencer had at least taught the young Diana the importance of keeping up appearances, something that would shape the rest of her life. Such an attitude ran in the family; it was the duty of the aristocracy. 'Remember you're a Spencer', the princess used to tell herself later at difficult moments in her marriage to bolster her confidence and self-esteem. It was a gift she mastered well. Paul Burrell, Diana's butler for a decade, remembers her remarkable ability to throw off feelings of depression or disappointment in order to take on her public persona as the smiling, confident Princess of Wales.

The Spencers had not always had money – various ancestors had sold off the family's heirlooms or petitioned monarchs for lucrative government positions in the colonies in order to raise essential funds. But they had always lived up to the duties and expectations of their social position as the leaders of Northamptonshire society. The 13,000 acres of the family home, Althorp (in one of those linguistic quirks nurtured by England's rural gentry, leaving outsiders floundering, it is invariably pronounced as 'Altrop') had been the playground and working land for the earls of Spencer for 500 years. Diana's father, Johnnie Spencer, was the heir to Althorp, along with its hundred tied cottages, its fine furniture, gallery of great paintings and collections of silver and porcelain; he would become the eighth earl on his father's death. He was acting as Master of the Royal Household when his daughter was born, having formerly served as an equerry to the Queen.

On the other side of the family, Diana's mother, Frances Roche, was the daughter of Lord and Lady Fermoy, respectively a former equerry to and friend of George VI and a lady-in-waiting and friend to the Queen Mother. The Fermoys had been given Park House on the royal estate at Sandringham – originally built to house guests for royal hunting weekends – to keep them close to the royal family. It was at Park House that Diana spent the first years of her life, her parents taking over the lease after the death of her grandfather.

This was the aristocratic tradition that shaped Diana's life. She would evolve into the people's princess, but she was a child of the aristocracy, and it was the rules of the aristocracy that she inherited. Chief among them, for a girl of her age, was romantic innocence. (This was the woman who, as an expectant mother, confided to a well-wisher that no one had warned her about morning sickness. One wonders what might have been the subject of late-night conversations in the dorms of Riddlesworth Hall and West Heath School, where Diana was educated with other girls of her own background.)

Of course, the blessing of innocence does not always mean protection from misery. The Spencers were an unconventional family and the Spencer children later recalled that they had a largely unhappy childhood. Because of their competitive natures and the differences in age between the two oldest daughters – Sarah and Jane – and Diana and her younger brother, the siblings were divided by tensions. Diana later became convinced that she had disappointed her parents because she was a girl – the third daughter – when they greatly wanted a boy who would become heir to the Spencer title. Her mother later conceded, 'Diana was born when a boy was much needed, much wanted, and not a girl', but denied that meant that the birth of a daughter was an anticlimax for her and her husband. She squarely blamed one of the spiritual counsellors with whom Diana later surrounded herself for planting that idea in her daughter's mind.

In 1967, Johnnie Spencer and his wife divorced. Diana's mother moved out to live with Peter Shand Kydd, a businessman who had made a fortune in the wallpaper industry, with whom she had begun an affair. The split and its acrimonious aftermath traumatized the seven-year-old girl, who later described how it had unsettled both her and her younger brother Charles, then four years old, and had made the tensions worse among the four siblings. She also speculated that it might be somehow behind the eating disorders suffered in adult life by her and her sister Sarah. Typically, she remembered that one of her earliest dilemmas concerned clothing: her father gave her a green dress to wear for a wedding and her mother gave her a white one. The child agonized over the choice in an attempt not to display favouritism.

The children remained close to both parents at the time, and credited Peter Shand Kydd's household, where they spent half of their holidays each year, with helping them grow up with a broader social experience than many aristocratic offspring. But having to balance the demands of both parents was a nightmare. Much of Diana's childhood was spent travelling between her parents' separate homes, or between either of their homes and school.

Worse came when Johnnie, by this time Earl Spencer, married Raine, Countess of Dartmouth, in July 1977. He gave his children no warning of his second marriage until it had taken place. The children's new stepmother, the daughter of the larger-than-life romantic novelist Barbara Cartland, was as unreal and unlikely a character as her mother, all bouffant hair and loud opinions, many of which she had formed while a Conservative member of the Greater London Council. When Diana and her brother Charles met her for the first time over lunch, they disliked her on sight.

Raine at once took charge of trying to reorganize the estate at Althorp to pay off the death duties of £2.25 million the eighth earl had inherited from his father. She fired many of the staff and began selling off some of the more valuable items from the collections of art and silver. Despite their father's stubborn defence of Raine's actions as essential to enable the upkeep of the house, the children found it impossible to forgive such a betrayal of their family's heritage. They began to copy county society in dubbing their stepmother 'Raine of Terror' and 'Acid Raine'.

After Earl Spencer died in 1992 – Raine had nursed him through a long illness after a stroke – there was a partial reconciliation between Diana and her stepmother. At the end of her life, Diana was estranged from her mother, who lived a reclusive life on a remote Scottish island. The estrangement was apparently the result of Diana's unwillingness to listen to her mother's advice, and reflected the princess's increasing determination to protect herself by surrounding herself only with those people who said what she wanted to hear. Another family rift was between Diana and her brother. Despite his provocative eulogy at Diana's funeral, Charles Spencer had largely lost his sister's trust after offering her a house on the Althorp estate as a much-needed country bolthole, and then, following Diana's acceptance, withdrawing the offer without explanation.

But in her youth, at least when she was away at school, Diana was free to indulge her love of animals by looking after the school's pets. Unlike her mother and her sister Sarah, however, she did not like horses, which she took against after an early riding accident. She was an unremarkable student and famously completed her schooling with only one O-level, but she established a reputation as a sportswoman, particularly strong in swimming and netball, and as a fine pianist and enthusiastic dancer.

The love of dance stayed with Diana throughout her life. Like many little girls, she harboured dreams of becoming a ballerina. Unlike most others, she had a whole country home to use as a studio, and would put on her black leotard to practise pliés and bar work, often starting before half past seven in the morning. She used the marble floor of the entrance hall at Althorp to practise tap dancing, drawing the curtains so that no one could see her and revelling in the echoing acoustics. Even after it became apparent that she would be too tall to be a ballet dancer – her brother Charles called the realization 'one of the early disappointments of her life' – she kept on dancing.

During the early years of her royal career she continued to have lessons, and the English National Ballet became one of the first charities she adopted. Peter Schaufuss, who was then artistic director of the company, described how the new princess enjoyed dancing with members of the company: 'I think she would return to that feeling that she had maybe when she was a younger girl and wanted to be a dancer. I think it was a kind of moment of relaxation and a moment of freedom, a moment of nonpressure maybe'. Surely the graceful movement and dignified posture of the princess, the seeming ease with which she could unfold her tall frame from the back of a car without making a clumsy move, owed much to the poise and grace she had learned as a dancer.

As a schoolgirl, Diana also attracted praise from her teachers for her kindness and consideration toward others. The caring side of her personality had emerged long before she became the Princess of Wales: she would enthusiastically look after her siblings at home, help friends at school and join in visits to hospitals. Again, such duties were in the blood of the class into which she had been born. For centuries it had been the accepted social round of the aristocracy to visit those in the village who were sick, to keep a paternal watch over those less fortunate who lived within their purview.

WHEN IT COMES TO CLOTHES, members of the aristocracy traditionally share a number of characteristics. One is an indifference to what people outside their immediate circle might think of their appearance, and a readiness to wear their country uniform even in the city. Another is, paradoxically, a consciousness of their position in society and the obligation to dress accordingly. What the nobility tend to possess is not fashion sense, but style. Take the example of Queen Elizabeth the Queen Mother, the only other non-royal before Diana to marry an

heir to the throne. She had long since learned what types of clothes flattered her and she stuck to them so faithfully as to make them her own, creating a look that was not only unique but with which she clearly felt comfortable. She made no attempt to follow fashion. Indeed, like her daughter the Queen, she seemed to be above fashion, that ever-moving flow of ideas and innovations endlessly accepted, changed, developed – and then rejected. Instead, she had her own personal style which endured long after seasonal fashion had died.

When she became Princess of Wales, Diana, too, had a kind of style, but of a far less assured and distinctive kind. For one thing, as the designer David Sassoon points out, she had been brought up with little money to spend on her wardrobe. Diana's clothes reflected the style of young women of her class and education, like her sisters. They belonged to the middle reaches of the aristocracy or the gentry and had been brought up among the county elite but then moved to London in search of diversion, marriage partners or employment. Perhaps they took a flat with their friends in Fulham, Earl's Court or Battersea, but they often spent the weekends at house parties in the country, watching polo matches, following the hunt, or going point to point racing.

The social commentator Peter York famously labelled such young women the 'Sloane Rangers', for their high concentration around Sloane Square, where the King's Road meets Chelsea proper. They were easily identifiable by their green Wellingtons and corduroys, sleeveless quilted jackets, high piecrust collars, round-necked sweaters and strings of pearls. They shopped on the King's Road, buying cashmere jerseys and Laura Ashley dresses, and for the most part dressed for the city as they did for the country, even wearing their Barbours in the heart of town. If they had much of an education beyond their public school, it was likely to be at a university such as Bristol or Exeter, from where it was easy to escape to the country. They worked for estate agents or auction houses, as cooks for boardrooms in the City – Diana did a Cordon Bleu cookery course – or as nannies. For many, work was more of a diversion than a necessity: many, like Diana and her two sisters, had been given flats in London by their parents and expected to have bills dealt with by the family estate or solicitors.

York's social archetype was a caricature, of course, but it spread like wildfire and became an instantly recognizable social type, like the crafty Cockney or the Scouse likely lad. The reason that the label stuck was that the

caricature had so much truth within it. London at the start of the Eighties did suddenly seem to be full of the offspring of country estates throughout the land, whose effortless social superiority endeared them to no one but their own kind. They were children of the families that had once run the British Empire, taking on offices in the Raj or filling the junior officer ranks of the Armed Services. After a few decades, they had found themselves embarrassed by their idleness and lack of purpose, but now the wind of political change that had brought Margaret Thatcher to power in 1979 gave them new licence to reclaim their position at the top of Britain's social tree. In turn, the rump of the gentry provided models for the crop of East End boys getting rich in the City, who wanted to legitimize their position in society by emulating their traditional social betters, patronizing their Saville Row tailors, drinking the same Cristal Champagne, buying polo ponies and dressing up for days out at Henley and Royal Ascot.

Diana became for the press the unofficial figurehead of Sloane Rangers everywhere when she became engaged to the heir to the throne. She was photographed at polo matches in corduroy knickerbockers, whimsically patterned knitwear and, inevitably, in the quintessential Sloane garment, the Barbour. She and her friends chatted and enjoyed picnics, or helped tread the divots back into the pitch between chukkas, and then climbed into their Golfs and Polos to drive back to Chelsea, Battersea or Clapham.

Ruffed blouses, pearls and floral skirts did not disappear from Diana's wardrobe for some time. One favourite print skirt was probably the item she wore most frequently during the early years of her marriage. Donald Campbell, who made clothes for Diana for the first five years of her marriage, observed the influence on the princess of her class and upbringing: 'For those people, fashion is very much down the line. They're told at a very early age, "Don't be vain about how you look, don't look in the mirror, because no one is going to be looking at you." She thought fashion was a necessary evil'.

The way that Diana and her peers dressed betrayed a complete disregard for their urban counterparts. When Diana moved into Coleherne Court in Earl's Court in 1977 – she shared her flat there with three friends from a similar background – London's fashion scene was already undergoing a seismic shift. Only a couple of years earlier, and only a half mile away, Vivienne Westwood and Malcolm McClaren had opened their shop Sex near World's End on the

King's Road. Westwood's experiments with ripped and pinned T-shirts, adapted bondage gear, and in-your-face icons of rebellion, allied with McClaren's genius for self-promotion, were the most visible sign of a whole new attitude to fashion.

Little of this made an impression on Lady Diana Spencer. She stuck to her accustomed uniform of inexpensive casual separates – light years away from what later became known as a fashion statement – for her work first as a nanny and later as a part-time assistant at the Young England kindergarten. It was at this point, after Diana had caught Charles's attention with her expressions of sympathy for the death of Lord Mountbatten, that the British caught their first real sight of the princess-to-be.

WHEN THE PRESS FOUND OUT about the new romance, they high-tailed it to Young England. Eventually, Diana agreed to a photo call – the first, and one of the worst managed, of her life. Dressed in purple and mauve separates with a sleeveless sweater, she stood against the sunlight, which shone through her thin summer skirt. She had chosen the skirt on purpose, because it was printed with tiny hearts. It was the first example of Diana using her wardrobe to convey a subtle message, but on this occasion it was so subtle that it was completely overlooked. The next day the papers were interested not in the dress itself, but in her legs silhouetted clearly against the sun. Such inadvertent exposure would have been embarrassing enough for any woman if someone had pointed it out on the street; the now iconic photo splashed all over the world's press caused a sensation. Prince Charles apparently commented, 'I knew your legs were good, but I didn't realize they were that spectacular'. But he also grumbled, 'But did you really have to show them to everybody?'

The prospective royal bride began her long apprenticeship in how to handle the press, marking the start of a complex but, on occasion, mutually beneficial relationship. (Once she persuaded one of the photographers to move her car when it was boxed into a tight parking space.) Photographer Jayne Fincher recalls staking out a house where Diana worked as a part-time nanny when the princess-to-be came out pushing a pram. 'Right', she told the press pack, 'I'm going for a walk now and I don't want you lot all running after me. But if you will behave, when I come back you'll be able to do some pictures then'. That was exactly what happened, and Fincher recalls, 'It was quite a thing to grasp for someone that young and inexperienced'.

Diana's playful banter with the press could go only so far. This remained the case throughout her life. She instinctively understood that such levity was not an option for her. She was light-hearted, with a clear sense of fun that resisted the restraints of royal behaviour, but she also had a sense of duty. She would be the mother of the next monarch and she knew that she must not let the side down. Such a sense of duty had been instilled in the Spencer family for generations and it informed everything that Diana did in public: how she appeared, what she said and what she wore.

TO BEGIN WITH, IT SEEMED that Diana could do little right when it came to what she wore. She knew very little about fashion, which is about display (although she did understand about clothes, which are concerned with ease, comfort and, above all for her class, suitability). The clothes she chose for her official engagement photographs barely fitted her; neither, as we have seen, did the black dress she wore for her first public appearance with her fiancé. In addition, the dressmakers to whom her mother introduced her were used to dressing people at least a generation older.

Fortunately, the bride-to-be had other guidance, from Felicity Clark, who was then beauty editor at British *Vogue*. Clark, who was a friend of the two older Spencer sisters – Sarah had worked as her assistant at the magazine – and had first met their younger sister when she was only fourteen, remembers that a number of people began mentioning to her socially that Diana showed signs of blossoming into a great beauty. They suggested that she include her in a regular *Vogue* feature, Portrait Portfolio, which highlighted possible faces of the future.

Clark tried to set up a photo shoot but Diana proved elusive, owing to her work, and the shoot kept being delayed. By the time Clark finally got the young woman into the studio with the consummate society portrait photographer Lord Snowdon, Diana was already being mentioned as a possible new partner for Prince Charles. Fortuitously, the issue featuring her eventually appeared on 24 February 1981, the very day on which the couple's engagement was announced.

*Vogue* photographed the young debutante wearing a cream organdie and lace dress by Gina Fratini, who already dressed Princess Margaret and Princess Anne, and had developed an understanding of royal clothes. For the published shot, however, Clark and the editor, Beatrix Miller, instead selected a photograph of Diana wearing a blush-pink ruffled chiffon blouse designed by a pair of young fashion graduates, David and Elizabeth Emanuel. Clark recalls that the princess loved anything with frills and ruffles, and felt that the shirt was highly feminine. Snowdon's first portrait – he would continue to photograph Diana throughout her life – showed her as what *Vogue* termed an English rose, with blushing cheeks and steady blue eyes and the merest hint of wistfulness.

Within a month or so, Clark found herself arranging another shoot with Snowdon, this time at Highgrove House, Prince Charles's residence in Gloucestershire, where the photographer took pictures for everything from postage stamps to official portraits. At a time of overwhelming excitement and change in her life, Diana felt comfortable with Snowdon – as he did with her. He was already a part of the family into which she would be marrying and, like her, had joined it from a safely aristocratic background. In some of the most successful images, she was dressed simply in a white shirt, leaning against a wall. Diana would move away from such simplicity as she made the effort to become more regal. Ironically, she and her designers would then spend a lifetime trying to return her to it.

At the request of Frances Shand Kydd, Clark and her colleagues began to advise Diana on her wardrobe. They were also the elite of Britain's fashion journalists, however, and they had a royal wedding to anticipate. In a special souvenir issue they invited many of the leading British designers, such as Zandra Rhodes and Gina Fratini, to prepare sketches for what they thought the royal wedding dress should be. Anna Harvey, the *Vogue* fashion editor who became Diana's closest fashion adviser, points out that the sketch submitted by the Emanuels was remarkably close to the dress they actually designed after they were commissioned. Leading up to the event, in the excitement and speculation about the dress, no one thought to put two and two together.

Clark also began to help Diana in other ways. For example, when the young woman went to Balmoral with her fiancé, she rang Clark in London asking her to send various things that she could not get hold of near the remote Scottish estate, particularly sun cream. Diana specified a brand from the popular chemist Boots, and remained faithful to certain Boots make-up lines until the end of her life. At the time, and until long after the wedding, Diana had no lady-in-waiting or private secretary, although there was a maid at Balmoral to

keep her room clean. The newcomer had wandered into the world of royalty with no support mechanism beyond her mother and the women at *Vogue* to help her create a public image, although the Windsors were well aware of its necessity for a royal personality. With hindsight, it is possible to see this lack of interest in how Diana presented herself as the first of many slights from Buckingham Palace. It was almost as if she were a brood mare: an inconvenient necessity rather than a genuinely welcome addition to one of the most extraordinary families of the twentieth century.

Bill Pashley, one of Frances Shand Kydd's dressmakers, made some clothes for Diana's trip to Scotland. He recalls that they included knickerbockers, a cape, some evening dresses and a few day suits. Most memorably, he made the dogtooth-checked suit in which Diana was photographed with Charles by the banks of the River Dee, looking slim and blissfully happy next to her kilted fiancé. Pashley's clothes are hardly notable – the calf-length straight skirt and buttoned blouson are conservative in style, and utterly suited to their environment – but that is their whole strength. They fit their purpose precisely, and in this it is tempting to see Frances Shand Kydd's influence. While it is true that the mother's dressmakers proved largely unable to meet the new fashion demands of her daughter's life as the Princess of Wales, Pashley and another of Shand Kydd's stalwarts, Donald Campbell, steered Diana through the early months by ensuring that any missteps would err on the side of caution.

It was at the photocall by the side of the Dee that a reporter asked the royal couple if they were in love. An obvious question, one might think, if a little ungracious when facing a newly engaged couple. The blushing Diana had a ready answer, 'Yes, of course', but the Prince's affirmation seemed somewhat more circumspect: 'Whatever love is', he added. In retrospect, this seems more than a qualification. Indeed, it has come to have rather sinister overtones, implying, as many observers have noted, that even at the time the prince was not as committed to the match as his much younger fiancée. However, that is not an interpretation borne out by the fashion designers who had contact with the royal couple around the time of their engagement and during the early years of their marriage, who report that they seemed very much in love.

If Prince Charles was not sure what love was, then his bride-to-be certainly thought she knew. It was something warm and exciting, a romantic vision of ball gowns in chiffons and silks, Champagne and beautiful flowers –

and endless pleasure. It was a young girl's idea of love, full of the warmth and security that she had lacked as a child. Diana's vision might have been naive, but it was certainly fixed and powerful.

Right from the start, the princess-to-be proved to have strong ideas of her own that often overrode all advice she might be given. The dressmaker Donald Campbell was highly experienced – he dressed Diana's sisters, as well as their mother – and knew that the clothes he was making were not suitable for a customer of Diana's age. He said, 'It's a myth that you can advise the royal family on what to wear. To be absolutely honest, she chose. I didn't advise. She just came in and started buying. I don't think there were many of the things she wore of mine that I would have chosen for her'.

DIANA'S WARDROBE GREW RAPIDLY from the day of her engagement, when she acknowledged that she owned one long dress, one silk shirt and one smart pair of shoes. Of all her new clothes, the outfit that chimed best with her idée fixe of romance was one that did not actually belong to her: the soft pink chiffon blouse by the Emanuels that she had worn for the initial *Vogue* photo-shoot. She asked Felicity Clark for the phone number of the Emanuels and then organized an appointment to see the rest of their collection.

Welshman David Emanuel had married Elizabeth, of mixed American and English parentage, in 1975, when they were in their early twenties. Both studied at the Royal College of Art, where their end-of-year show in 1977 caused enough interest for them to feel sufficiently confident to open a business under their own name – most unusually for newly graduated fashion designers. Things were not easy. Quickly abandoning their wholesale business, they began to concentrate on what they called 'specials': one-off couture, ball and wedding gowns made from yard upon yard of lace, taffeta, organza and tulle. These were the sorts of things that a truly commercial fashion business treats with caution. Rightly or not, they are seen as the outward and visible signs of a label unlikely to attract much attention from press, store buyers or the general public.

Both of the Emanuels had independently received work experience in the studio of Roland Klein, whose training at Dior and as assistant to Karl Lagerfeld had made him one of London's greatest exponents of the art of cut, the basis of all couture. Klein, who went on to dress the Princess of Wales extensively himself, recalls that both designers were popular and evidently

skilled. His memory is that it was Elizabeth who had a tendency toward theatrical glamour – she later concentrated on the couple's evening wear – while David took a more understated approach toward daywear.

The Emanuels' clothes fitted perfectly with Diana's Hollywood view of romance and the princess and the designers hit it off at once. David recalls: 'She was fresh, with beautiful skin and clear, sparkling blue eyes, and fun; a bit leggy and gawky, because she was young'.

The relationship was almost stopped in its tracks, however, by Diana's ill-advised first purchase. This was the revealing black taffeta ball gown that she wore for her first official engagement, when photographs of her nearly falling out of her dress displaced details of the budget from the front pages of the newspapers. It had been hanging in the Emanuels' showroom, having already been worn once (by the actress Liza Goddard), when Diana urgently needed something formal. The furore sparked by photographs of the strapless gown marked the recognition that Diana's 'Sloane Ranger' image – cords, sweaters and pearls – did not tell the whole story. This young woman had the potential to become a glamorous addition to the royal family who would bring something that it had lacked for many years: sex appeal.

Diana, as we have seen, would wait a long time before she again wore black on a public occasion. But the dress was another signal of her determination to live out her fairytale and a sign that perhaps the fairytale was not so naive as it appeared. Above all, the black dress hinted that this was a young woman who craved sophistication, who craved womanhood.

THERE WAS GREAT PRESS SPECULATION about who would be commissioned to design the dress for the royal wedding. Every society dressmaker in London wanted the job, and at various times virtually all of them were mentioned in connection with it: Bill Pashley, who had designed wedding dresses for the two older Spencer sisters; Bellville Sassoon, the most experienced of all royal dressmakers; Gina Fratini at Hartnell, who later noted, 'I was sad that I didn't get the wedding dress; everyone expected me to'. But, with hindsight, it seems clear that there was only ever one likely choice for the commission. Diana loved the Emanuels' romantic vision, she loved the informality of their Brook Street showroom and their youth – they were only eight years older than her. Perhaps she also wanted to make a diplomatic acknowledgement of the principality of which she was about to become the princess by hiring a Welsh designer. The Emanuels it was, and the decision would have as ambivalent an outcome for the designers as the fairytale would for the princess.

Couturiers throughout London were disappointed – and then critical. Their faultfinding would resurface after the wedding, and continues today. The press, meanwhile, generally reacted with astonishment to the commission, claiming again and again that the Emanuels were 'unknowns'. This was largely true from the perspective of commercial fashion, but their label had been established for five years, and they had already dressed both the Duchess of Kent and Princess Michael of Kent. They were, however, inexperienced in designing clothes for major public events. They found it more than a little disconcerting to discover that there would be virtually no direction from the Palace. There were no official guidelines. The Royal Press Officer, Michael Shea, called the Emanuels to say 'Whatever you're doing, just keep on doing it'.

In fairness to the Palace, it should be remembered that the Queen and the Queen Mother had always relied on experienced couturiers – Hardy Amies and Norman Hartnell, respectively – for their image. When the Princess of Wales's wedding dress received a great deal of profession criticism, a Hartnell vendeuse said very sniffily to the author, 'She should have come to us. We know about such things'.

BEHIND CLOSED DOORS AND IN GREAT SECRECY – while journalists searched through the rubbish bins outside the workroom to try to find scraps of the fabric – the young Emanuels and their client began to work on a dress that would live up to the romance of what was already being billed as 'a fairy-tale wedding'. The designers closed their workroom for the four months of the commission and set about showing Diana their existing collection while drawing up new designs based on her preferences. They produced more than fifty different sketches based on the essential shape of a shoulder frill, tight waist and huge skirt.

There was a lot of fun and informality. The princess and the designers sat on the floor as they sorted through the drawings. The final design had full sleeves, and a balloningly full skirt reminiscent of Victorian cartoons in *Punch* poking fun at the foolishness of the 'fair sex' and the impracticality of high

fashion in general. When they moved on to the next stage and began to stitch toiles (models of the basic dress shape for fitting), they found that Diana was losing weight rapidly. She had lost a stone and a half by the time of the wedding, falling from a size 14 to a size 10. (Like everyone else at the time, they put down the weight loss to pre-wedding nerves rather than the effects of the bulimia from which Diana later revealed she suffered.) To keep up with her changing figure, the Emanuels had to make a series of toiles, each with a smaller bodice to compensate for the bride's shrinking stomach and bust.

The setting for the occasion, St Paul's Cathedral, was a huge space with a grand flight of steps up to the entrance. Diana and her designers felt it called for something suitably dramatic in order to make an impression. They joked about increasing the length of the train, making it bigger and bigger until it became, at twenty-five-feet long, almost totally overwhelming. It was hand embroidered with 10,000 mother-of-pearl sequins and pearls, which embroiderer Peggy Umpelby secretly stitched in place at her home. The gown itself required forty-five feet of ivory silk taffeta, provided by the weaver Stephen Walters, who had also woven silk for the gown in which Elizabeth II was crowned. One of the Emanuels' seamstresses, Nina Missetzis, made the whole dress in a locked room.

Meanwhile, the Emanuels had consulted another royal dressmaker, Maureen Baker, who had made the wedding dress for Princess Anne, the Princess Royal. On her advice they incorporated details to fulfil the old superstitions about marriage, providing Diana with things old, new, borrowed and blue. They sewed a tiny blue bow into the back of the dress and ordered new lace to trim the gown and silk from Dorset for the veil, as well as commissioning a tiny gold horseshoe, which they sewed into the label of the dress. The central panel of the front of the dress contained the 'old' – a piece of Carrickmacross lace that had belonged to Queen Mary, given to Diana by the Royal School of Needlework. Diana borrowed the Spencer family diamond tiara – the Emanuels trimmed the underside with velvet so that it could comfortably hold in place the bride's veil and train – and a pair of diamond earrings from her mother.

The rest of the princess's appearance was in the hands of make-up artist Barbara Daly and hairdresser Kevin Shanley. Daly was a pioneer at a time when there were few make-up specialists – she had trained at the BBC before being picked up by Grace Coddington for fashion shoots for *Vogue*. Felicity Clark had used her as the make-up artist on Diana's *Vogue* photographic shoots before the princess asked her to do the make-up on her wedding day. The two women hit it off immediately – Diana said to the equally tall Daly, 'It's great to meet someone I can look in the eye' – beginning a friendship that lasted for more than sixteen years. Daly found Diana a quick learner: she would apply make-up to half of her face then leave Diana to repeat the exercise to make the rest of her face match.

Daly recalls how naturally pretty Diana was, with her tendency to blush, intense blue eyes and noticeably good bone structure, which meant that there were few angles from which the young woman did not photograph well. But Diana did have, she also noticed, an unusual nose with something of a bump in the middle. As the two women worked together over the following years, Daly kept trying to insist that Diana give up her tendency to use too much eyeliner, which made her eyes, already startling, too large and heavy. She used to threaten to burn Diana's eyeliner pencils and on one shoot, she recalls, confiscated a number of eyeliners from Diana's bag. The princess excused herself and left the room, coming back in with liner around her eyes, and laughingly confessing, 'I had a pencil in the bedroom'.

For the wedding day, Daly's challenge was to create a make-up design that must last all day, with few opportunities for touch-ups, and that would look good in a number of different lights, from the interior of St Paul's to the balcony at Buckingham Palace. Diana would also have to photograph well under flashlights.

Unlike Barbara Daly, Kevin Shanley had not come through *Vogue*. He was already Diana's hairdresser at Head Lines, her regular hair salon, and was responsible for the much-imitated Diana bob of the princess's early royal career. He became Diana's first personal hairdresser and travelled with her on numerous official trips, but *Vogue* had serious misgivings about whether he would be able to adapt to the special demands of the wedding day.

Felicity Clark recalls advising Diana to use Michael from Michaeljohn for the task. She made an appointment for the two to meet, but Diana felt it would be disloyal to Shanley if she changed. Michael, Clark insists, had more experience working with tiaras, having already styled the hair of Princess Anne and Princess Alexandra. Unlike Shanley, he would have known how to weave

the hair around the velvet band of the tiara to keep it in place and to allow the diamonds to shine out more. Shanley's style of cutting was undeniably more natural, but in Clark's view it sat badly with the formal clothes, and the effect of the tiara was greatly reduced.

ON THE MORNING OF THE WEDDING, the Emanuels, Barbara Daly and Kevin Shanley all gathered early at Clarence House, the Queen Mother's residence, where Diana had spent her last night as a single woman. Daly remembers finding her in her bedroom watching breakfast TV footage of the crowds outside on the Mall. Diana joked, 'It's an awful lot of fuss for one little girl, isn't it?' The Queen Mother herself popped in at one point to see how things were going. Once the princess was dressed – she later spilled scent on the front of her gown while she was playing with her bridesmaids, but was too frightened to tell the Emanuels – Daly and the designers were whisked off by car to the cathedral, so that they could be there when Diana's carriage arrived. It was one of Daly's duties, while she touched up the princess's make-up before she left the cathedral at the end of the service, to use a pair of scissors to cut off the lower part of Diana's veil to reveal her face. Trying to throw the veil back over the bride's head might have had unpredictable consequences and the risk of anything going wrong had to be minimized.

But before the ceremony had even begun, almost as soon as the carriage door opened and the crowds roared their appreciation of the fairytale princess who climbed out, the carping began in the fashion world. The fabric had become creased on the journey across London – the Emanuels admit that they had underestimated the effects of the train being squashed into the cramped coach – and the dress looked less than pristine. As Anna Harvey observes, 'It was beautiful fabric, stunning, but to Joe Public, it looked as if it was made of creased brown paper'. Gina Fratini, who would have liked to design the dress herself, later said, 'I certainly would have known what fabric would crease or not'.

Roland Klein takes a more considered view. He admits that the Emanuels probably were not ready for the responsibility of the occasion, and that they failed to grasp the implications of the dress – not only its significance, but also more practical details such as how it would survive the journey. He says, 'It wasn't properly designed. It wasn't thought out properly'. In business terms, while it brought the Emanuels a lot of exposure and attracted a lot of custom, it also represented a high point from which their careers never really recovered.

But, Klein perceptively points out, the main problem with the dress was that it was too much of its time. The puffy sleeves and the huge skirts reflected the essential fashionable look of the early Eighties, when romantic excess was closely associated with glamour. The dress was too fashionable: it belonged so much to the time that it now looks dated. As Klein argues, court dress cannot be a fashion statement. If one of the royal ladies is photographed in 1950, people have to be able to look at the wedding photographs in the 1980s and beyond and not laugh out loud. But Klein admits that when he heard that the dress was being dry cleaned in Lilliman and Cox in Bruton Place, opposite his boutique, he rushed over to see it. And he concedes, 'The embroideries were exquisite. It was fabulously well made'.

Diana was later claimed to have said of the dress, 'I hope the moths get it'. If true, the sentiment almost certainly reflects more her feelings about her marriage than about her wedding gown, no matter how dated it may have become. It is as impossible to imagine the woman she became wearing the Emanuels' dress – arguably the most famous wedding gown in history – as it is to imagine the fresh-faced (though exhausted) bride in Lord Litchfield's official wedding photographs maturing into the sleek, elegant international style icon that she had become before her death.

But on that July day in 1981, after months of uncertainty in the fashion world, the new princess had beguiled the nation with her nursery vision of what it was like to become a princess. She struck an answering chord in romantics everywhere, thanks to the support of the Emanuels, Barbara Daly and others. Diana showed as much savvy in her relationship with them as she had already shown with the press. She was naturally appreciative and always scrupulously polite. She had already learned that the creation of her own personal style could not be an individual effort.

That evening, at the end of what she had found an exhausting day, she telephoned both the Emanuels and Barbara Daly to thank them for their help. Daly was sitting at home when the phone rang soon after nine o'clock and a voice said, 'Hello, it's Diana. I wanted to thank you and just to talk to you'. The two women chatted about the day, and Daly was flattered that the princess was taking the time, though also a little sad that the new bride clearly felt the

need for a supportive chat. This was not the last time: whenever Diana was feeling a little wistful, she turned to the people she trusted most, and these were more often than not the people who helped create and maintain her image rather than the stiff and strange family into which she had married.

THE WINDSORS HAD SECURED the requisite dynastic marriage to ensure the continuation of the royal succession. A prince had found his bride, and a girl with little experience of the world had stepped into an alien orbit in which it would take her years to find herself again. Obscured from view by the sequins and billowing meringue of the 'perfect' wedding dress lay problems and misery. Within little more than a decade, both marriages behind the creation of the dress had collapsed. Both the princess and her designers would learn that to live in a fairytale takes more than dressing like a fairytale princess. It was a hard lesson for them all.

**She was fresh, with**

beautifu

**clear, sparkling**

a bit leggy anc

because

skin and
**blue eyes, and fun;**
gawky,
she was young.

DAVID EMANUEL

# diana's **shoes**

Prior to her engagement, Diana owned only one smart pair of shoes and was often as comfortable in green Wellingtons. But as her wardrobe became more formal and organized, her shoes followed suit. In the early years, she wore sensible flats and low-heeled court shoes, not only to fit in with the conservative royal image, but also so as not to dwarf Charles. These Jimmy Choo flat-heeled pumps with the trademark 'V' cut into the top Diana called her 'regulars', and she had many pairs in different colours.

Diana remained loyal to Jimmy Choo throughout all the stages of her fashion evolution. He created hundreds of pairs of shoes for her, from flats to more glamorous high heels, always combining elegance with practicality. A pair of freshly completed beige ballerina flats was due to be delivered to Diana on the Monday after her death. The designer would keep the shoes in his workshop as a memento of a special client and friend.

Diana loved shoes and had hundreds of pairs, which were meticulously sorted in colour order beneath the clothes hanging on the rails in her walk-in dressing room at Kensington Palace. Diana's shoes were designed to match a particular outfit in colour and sometimes pattern, and many of her shoes were bespoke, made for special occasions. To ensure that the shoes matched her outfit perfectly, a sample of the fabric would be given to the shoemaker. Nonetheless, Diana often wore her shoes on more than one occasion. Such was the case with these classic high-heeled Chanel courts, which are typical of her later, sleeker style.

For Diana, there were only two shoemakers in London. One was the Malaysian-born Jimmy Choo, the other was Spanish-born Manolo Blahnik, whose Chelsea store became a virtual place of pilgrimage for fashionable ladies during the Eighties and Nineties. As Diana's wardrobe became more daring after she separated from Charles, so her heels became higher and her shoes more glamorous and feminine. High heels and sexy straps, such as these silver Jimmy Choos, elongated her already-long legs, pushing her bottom back and her chest out to make the most of her toned figure. Both Choo and Blahnik used their understanding of balance and anatomy to create daring and sexy shoes that were also comfortable and easy to walk in.

'And then this young girl came along and brightened up the royal family... She could give any supermodel or actress a run for her money.'

JACQUES AZAGURY

# creating **a style**

In the fairy story, the ugly duckling has to hide away through a long, lonely winter before becoming a beautiful swan. Diana Spencer was never an ugly duckling, but at the time of her engagement she was nothing like the swan she would become – elegant, sophisticated, every woman's ideal of glamour, every man's secret crush. The later Diana developed, in the words of Jacques Azagury, every couture designer's perfect figure – tall and lean, but broad shouldered and with a fine bust. Azugury, whose eighteen dresses for Diana included some of her most memorable outfits, recalls, 'She was the only customer I got really excited about'.

That was a long way in the future, and almost inconceivable in Diana's early public life, when the papers dubbed her 'Shy Di' and *Vogue* magazine said of her engagement that it was 'rather as if a charming young giraffe had wandered into the royal enclosure'. The shy and confused teenager had no chance to mature into the Princess of Wales in private; her transformation had to take place not just in public, but also in the face of the largest collection of camera lenses ever assembled.

The royal family, of course, has generations of experience of how to present itself. Clothes have been part of the way in which monarchs have reinforced their importance in the eyes of their subjects since Henry VIII and Elizabeth I commissioned paintings of themselves adorned in their most

imposing royal costumes. What Henry required from Hans Holbein the Younger and Elizabeth from Nicholas Hilliard was a display of their rank and status. In a modern constitutional monarchy, the requirements of royal dressing are somewhat reduced, of course. Apart from formal occasions, such as the state opening of Parliament, royal dress is much the same as that of any other members of the Establishment. Although clothes have to separate the royal family from the rest of us – to reinforce the difference in status – they cannot risk alienating people with overt displays of social superiority. For the royal men, well-cut suits (always from Saville Row) invariably have become the choice on occasions that do not require military uniform. For the Queen, impeccable daywear and evening dresses, accented with jewellery from the greatest private collection in the world, are such standard tools of the trade that she would describe these pieces to Norman Hartnell, who made many of them, as her 'uniform'. They were as much part of a regulated public appearance as any military uniform.

In an equally telling piece of monarchical shorthand, the Queen also refers to her official clothes as 'props'. The role of the modern royal family is nothing if not theatrical, and all royal designers have to be aware of the need to balance couture and costume. Diana would prove herself easily the most effective of the family in this aspect of royal behaviour. Years later, when she had announced her withdrawal from many of her official duties after her divorce from Prince Charles, Diana bumped into the actor Jeremy Irons and asked him what he was doing. Irons replied that he was taking a year off from acting. Diana replied, 'So am I'.

When Diana became part of the royal family, the Queen asked Lady Susan Hussey, a senior lady-in-waiting, to mentor the young princess in some of the rules of royal dress. Anne Beckwith-Smith, Diana's own principal lady-in-waiting and personal secretary from the time of her marriage, was another source of advice. The rules are few, and largely common sense: wear bold tones so that people can see you; put weights in the hems of dresses so that they will not rise up in the wind; reinforce points of dresses to carry the weight of brooches. (Although Diana was not a great fan of brooches, she was on certain occasions obliged to wear orders, such as the Royal Family Order. The miniature portrait of the Queen surrounded by diamonds on a chartreuse-yellow silk band was heavy enough to pull or even rip a normal evening gown.)

When your profession is based almost entirely on your public appearance, as it would be for Diana, how to dress is one of the most vital tricks of the trade. As Diana herself summed it up: 'You'd be amazed what one has to worry about. You've got to put your arm out to get some flowers, so you can't have something too revealing, and you can't have hems too short because when you bend over, there are six children looking up your skirt'. Like other young socialites who have been to finishing school in Switzerland – Diana herself was so homesick that she left after a month – she had learned how to strategically place a handbag or a shawl over her lap or bust when getting into or out of a car in a short skirt or wearing a top that was liable to fall forward.

But already during the royal engagement, it had become clear that Diana was an unprecedented phenomenon in the royal family. The press interest in her was intense. From the start, the focus on her clothes, her hair and her make-up outweighed any such attention given to the Queen, Princess Anne or any of the other royal women since Wallis Simpson or the young Princess Margaret. Diana's natural attractiveness, her shyness and diffidence, and her English prettiness – a mixture of innocence and gaucherie – ensured that she would always draw the eye of the public and the press. There were just enough 'girl-next-door' elements in her appearance for people to identify with her. She was seen as neither 'posh' nor overprivileged – even though, with her noble lineage, she was both.

Jacques Azagury sums up the arrival of the new princess: 'Since Princess Margaret in the Sixties, there had never been a show person in the monarchy for British fashion. And then this young girl came along and brightened up the royal family... She could give any supermodel or actress a run for her money'.

DIANA TURNED FOR ADVICE TO *VOGUE* MAGAZINE – British fashion's equivalent of royalty – an institution published from very chic headquarters in Hanover Square in Mayfair. At that time edited by Beatrix Miller, *Vogue* to some extent was British fashion. If anything was going on in the fashion world then *Vogue* not only knew about it but in one way or another would be involved, for the magazine took very seriously its self-assumed brief to nurture and promote British fashion. The women who staffed *Vogue* were striking in themselves, impeccably presented and socially accomplished, and often from the same circles as Diana herself.

# JACQUES AZAGURY

Her association with *Vogue* beauty editor Felicity Clark had borne fruit, but it became clear that the princess needed the advice of a fashion specialist in order to focus her style into a statement. The task fell to Anna Harvey, *Vogue*'s elegant fashion editor, a senior journalist who knew as much about British fashion as anyone in London. Harvey would become Diana's guide to the world of fashion and, even after Diana had made herself the unquestioned mistress of that world, would remain a long-term collaborator and facilitator.

Gracious, patrician and modest, Harvey was perfectly suited to the role, although, characteristically, she continues to play down her own importance, saying, 'I was definitely the messenger rather than the leader'. She was responsible for bringing together possible wardrobe choices for a woman who might have to change her clothes five times in a day and yet did not have the freedom to go shopping or the time to keep up with everything that was happening in British fashion. Anna Harvey gathered drawings, produced sample garments for Diana to try on, liaised with designers to request outfits for particular occasions, and introduced new creators to the process as and when they were needed. But she was far more than the kind of glorified personal shopper that her characteristic understatement implies. She not only obtained Diana's clothes, but also played a vital role in their judicious selection. In the partnership, Harvey came to fill the role of a kind of doorkeeper, enabling access to the princess only for those designers she thought would give Diana what she wanted.

To do that, she had to understand the princess's needs and personal tastes implicitly, because Diana was not a person to have clothes pushed on her. Harvey recalls one incident in which she urged Diana to buy a double-breasted grey flannel coat that she thought would suit her. About a year later, Diana handed her a carrier bag and said, 'Anna, this is a present for you. I know you like it'. Inside was the unworn coat. It was the princess's gracious way of letting the other woman know that, despite its suitability as fashion, for her the coat had been a mistake. It is a testament to the closeness of the two women that their relationship lasted sixteen years, until Diana's death, even though to begin with, Harvey was not allowed to meet the princess. She would call in clothes to the *Vogue* office, where Felicity Clark and a fitter would carry out a fitting behind closed doors. Inevitably, the process proved unsatisfactory on both sides. Eventually Diana observed, 'I think it might be better if Anna was here'.

ONE OF HARVEY'S FIRST PROJECTS involved the preparation of the trousseau for the royal honeymoon. She remembers that *Vogue* was given details of the destinations of the royal yacht *Britannia*, aboard which the newlyweds would spend part of their honeymoon, in order to put together a suitable wardrobe.

Also influential in the preparation of the trousseau was Frances Shand Kydd, who later recalled, 'I did what a mother does on these occasions. I took her to fashion houses and a number of shops in London where I felt comfortable, and which provided clothes that she liked wearing'. Donald Campbell was one such; he produced a pretty dress with flower motifs suitable for the sunshine on the cruise. In response to criticism that the princess was dressing older than her age, Mrs Shand Kydd observed, 'All children pick up something from their mothers, but I was simply there to introduce her to certain designers and she took it from there'.

The press was full of speculation about Diana's going-away outfit. Again, the princess had fallen back not on *Vogue* but on her mother's recommendation, and ordered a dress from Bellville Sassoon. It was only when the princess-to-be entrusted Anna Harvey with a swatch of the dress fabric to take to Manolo Blahnik in Old Church Street in Chelsea to have shoes made that the journalist realized the weight of trust that Diana had placed in her – and the even greater need for secrecy. The going-away outfit itself was in a colour that Diana insisted on – she referred to it as cantaloupe, but it was actually a very pale apricot shade – with a sophisticated straight skirt. In an early example of the practicality for which she later became renowned, the princess ordered the outfit with two jackets, with short and long sleeves respectively, to be prepared for any kind of weather.

Although there are countless stories of Diana making shopping expeditions to Selfridges or of simply stopping her car outside a boutique if she was particularly struck by something in the window, the relations between Diana and her dressmakers were managed more often than not by a series of discreet phone calls from Vogue House. When Diana arrived at the *Vogue* office, she parked in the basement garage and took the back lift to the fifth floor, where Beatrix Miller had her office. Harvey made sure that there were racks and racks of clothes and boxes of shoes and accessories for the excited princess to look through. She recalls, 'I don't think that she originally had any idea how many lovely things there were out there. Her enthusiasm was contagious'.

Once, Diana turned up to select clothes in the pale lemon-yellow dungarees that she wore off-duty many times around 1981. There could be few more symbolic contrasts than the clash between the private world of Diana's own favourite clothing and the high fashion world of public dressing to which she was being introduced.

Harvey's brief was simple. For formal occasions the princess was expected to wear British designers – and with the exception of a few notable occasions abroad when she selected clothes as a compliment to her hosts, she always did so when she was on official business. And she needed clothes that fitted their purpose – lots of them. The new princess was embracing a lifestyle that was essentially straight out of the Regency pleasure garden or the Victorian parlour, with up to four changes of clothes a day and strict etiquette about what could be worn when. For example, it was the custom of the royal family to dress for tea even when on holiday in Balmoral. While in private she tended to prefer cashmere jumpers and jackets worn over soft pleated skirts, Diana needed a full range of suits and evening dresses for official duties. She once likened the experience to taking the care needed to dress for a wedding every day.

Working out the protocols of dressing as a princess inevitably involved a certain amount of trial and error. Diana's early wardrobe was generally too fussy, too startling in its primary colours and too middle-aged with its pussycat bows and feathered hats. But one can hardly lay the blame for such fashion failures at Anna Harvey's door, or indeed at that of the princess herself. They reflected the weight of hundreds of years of royal and aristocratic tradition, which showed itself in dictates that demanded, for example, that a hat be worn for public appearances, almost always with gloves. Such traditions had a basis in common sense. The hat was not only a crown substitute, but also prevented hair flying around in the wind, just as gloves protected hands that would have to shake those of many, many people every day, many of them sweaty with nerves.

Diana and her advisers had to marry such practical considerations with the aspirations and enthusiasm of a young woman with a highly romantic idea of what a princess should be and how a sophisticated princess should dress. Diana's mother was still a far stronger influence than any outsiders, no matter how professionally skilled they were. It was Mrs Shand Kydd who introduced Diana to the milliner John Boyd, originally from Scotland, who produced the notoriously successful Princess Diana feathered hat with a gently curving brim.

The Scotsman's collaboration with the princess almost single-handedly revived the fashion of wearing hats among young British bourgeoise women. Boyd was an experienced royal milliner, having made hats for Princess Michael of Kent, and for Princess Anne since she was seventeen years old. He knew the demands of creating hats to match a range of outfits, that could photograph well from all angles and that did not obscure the face of the wearer. He also made hats for the then prime minister, Margaret Thatcher, whom he used to visit for fittings at Downing Street at eight o'clock in the morning. Boyd put Princess Diana in small hats that revealed her trademark fringe, often with the tiny veil that became a part of her early style. Boyd's most successful look made a spectacular appearance with Bellville Sassoon's cantaloupe going-away outfit: he topped a small hat with a cantaloupe Prince of Wales ostrich feather in a witty acknowledgement of Diana's new royal status.

THE BRITISH HAD NOT EXACTLY BEEN WORRYING about the arrival of a future heir to the throne, but the union somehow seemed to personify the nation's need for a feel-good story and it boosted to new heights the popularity of the royal family. Magazines and newspapers dedicated to the Windsors saw their sales soar. It also very soon became clear that Diana sold – not only newspapers but also memorabilia, clothes and hats. For every woman who had loved someone unattainable, for every child from a broken home, for everyone who felt awkward and shy, Diana's story was a true romance. Wedding memorabilia filled shops and front rooms with a pride and cheerfulness far removed from its current forlorn reappearances at provincial car boot sales.

The media determined that Diana was to be the saviour of the royal family by pointing a way into the twenty-first century. It did so because that was what readers wanted: a new style of royal, more accessible, and at the same time prettier and more glamorous. Fleet Street still had power then, in the days before twenty-four-hour news, satellite TV and the plethora of specialist fashion magazines. And *The Sun*, the *Mirror*, the *Express* and above all the *Mail* knew how to make the best of the opportunity, for themselves and the royal family. The *Daily Mail* dressed Diana 'look-alikes' in Sloane Ranger uniforms of corduroy knickerbockers and ruffled shirts. It called the feature 'Follow the Leader'.

Diana was clearly a fashion icon even in the early days, when many fashion cognoscenti were throwing up their hands in horror at her sartorial naiveté.

The Lady Diana hat, which became firmly established as one of the princess's favourites after her husband reportedly complimented her on a bonnet she wore for the Trooping of the Colour ceremony in 1981, struck an answering chord throughout Middle England. Soon the shelves of Chelsea Girl and Miss Selfridge were full of small bonnets with absurdly dyed plumage, and the announcement of another summer wedding sent birds flapping for cover. So many wedding photographs from the early Eighties are now sadly dated by the Diana hats, puffed sleeves or puritan collars that it must be worth asking: why did Diana's fashion influence spread so widely so quickly on such flimsy evidence?

The first answer, of course, is fame. Fame has its own glamour, and royal fame, which cannot be bought into, potentially has the most glamour of all. After more than a decade of virtually constant media speculation, the heir to the throne was finally getting married. The announcement of the engagement was a fillip to a nation that had become dulled during a decade of high unemployment and inflation. It was romantic and reassuring. David Sassoon remembers that after Diana wore what became known as the Gonzaga dress in November 1981, hundreds of children wrote to her because it was exactly what they thought a princess should look like.

The couture house Bellville Sassoon was perhaps the most consistent of Diana's early designers, understanding precisely what was required for the new royal. Opened by former debutante Belinda Bellville in 1953, but carried on after her retirement by David Sassoon, whom she had recruited as a student from the Royal College of Art, Bellville Sassoon was based in a small store near the King's Road in Chelsea. The Gonzaga dress was named for its appearance at the 1981 opening of a London exhibition of the treasures of the Italian family who had ruled Renaissance Mantua. It was a gossamer creation that blended soft blues and pinks with subtle silver beading and a feminine off-the-shoulder neckline, gathered by a blue satin sash around the waist. Although nothing if not modest, it exposed Diana's shoulders and slender neck, which she highlighted by wearing a multi-strand pearl choker reminiscent of those chosen by Princess Alexandra in the early years of the twentieth century.

Like the Emanuels' wedding gown, the Bellville Sassoon Gonzaga dress had more than a touch of the fairytale about it. It struck a chord with the public, and also with the young girl feeling out her new role, who returned to it a number of times. A year later, when the dress reappeared at the premiere of the

1981

movie *Gandhi*, Diana wore it with a striking pendant with a design of Prince of Wales feathers. Two years later, the princess wore the dress again for a Royal Command Performance in London.

Anna Harvey saw clearly the task facing the princess and her own role in it. She says, 'We had to find a middle way between the pie-crust collared blouse and the catwalk'. 'At least', she recalls, 'there were a lot of people making quite proper clothes'. British dressmakers of the time fell into two camps. There were those who largely mistook flamboyance and undirected innovation for a creative vision. Their fashion shows made the headlines but they almost entirely failed to realize their potential. But there were others who stuck to doing the basics well; they might sacrifice a certain amount of originality, but they produced stylish clothes, well cut and made, with an expertise based on centuries of fine tailoring for women as well as men.

Harvey had a wide choice: Caroline Charles and Jan Vanvelden, for example, were up-market designers who made clothes that were perfectly suited to the few dressy public occasions, such as Ascot or Henley, still enjoyed by the British upper classes. Gina Fratini, Zandra Rhodes and Murray Arbeid were skilled practitioners, like Bellville Sassoon. Fratini and Rhodes specialized in highly feminine clothes that fitted perfectly into the world of the fairytale princess, with pearl-beaded or hand-painted chiffons or organza trimmed with lace. Anna Harvey was also instrumental in finding suitable designers among London's young guns: Jasper Conran, Bruce Oldfield and Jacques Azagury were all producing striking formal and informal wear.

The French-born Roland Klein, a doyen of London fashion, received a telephone call from Harvey during the princess's engagement, after she had seen his collection and thought that Diana might be interested in viewing some of his designs. One of his casual outfits became a firm favourite of the princess and characterized her off-duty style: it was a simple, pleated, white linen skirt twinned with a white cotton sweater with a blue trompe-l'oeil scarf knitted into it. The princess was also widely photographed in a long off-the-shoulder dress in burgundy taffeta, with a puffy skirt typical of the time. Klein recalls that 'The dress became an instant success. Every store in the country kept reordering it. We called it the Di dress. We literally sold hundreds and hundreds'.

It was Klein's first brush with princess power. He remembers 'She was very influential. She put London fashion and London designers in front of the public at large. When she was wearing something that was photographed, it had an immediate effect'. Diana's other designers agreed. Murray Arbeid recalls, 'She was the greatest ambassadress for London fashion'.

It was clear already that the new princess had the potential to be a promotional force for British fashion such as had not been seen since the pop-star-inspired clothing of Swinging London in the Sixties. It was not only the designers who actually dressed the princess that benefited. The rag trade was as quick and ingenious as ever in exploiting the possibility to find new sales. There were cheap versions everywhere of what became Diana's early trademarks: puritan collars, flat-heeled pumps – the princess was always afraid of towering over her husband, who stood only an inch taller than she – pussycat bows in candy stripes, and the distinctive John Boyd hat.

It was reported that the enthusiasm for pumps like Diana's enabled a Northern Ireland factory to fight off the threat of closure simply by fulfilling demand for thousands of pairs a week. The effect of Diana's fondness for hats was credited with reinvigorating the whole British millinery industry. Likewise, the clutch bag that she carried as she left for her honeymoon became a bestselling accessory. When Diana carried a muff to visit Gloucester Cathedral on the coldest day of 1981 – it complemented a blue flannel, astrakhan-trimmed, Cossack-style coat by Bellville Sassoon – Harrods received record numbers of requests for what previously had been considered a rather unfashionable accessory.

Jewellery was another favourite for the copyists. Diana's sapphire-and-diamond engagement ring was copied in a whole range of materials, from cheap coloured glass to versions with real sapphires that cost almost as much as the original. The multi-strand pearl choker worn at the wedding also appeared in a whole range of prices.

When Roland Klein first began dressing his new customer during her engagement, he recalls that she would happily just pop in to the boutique on Tyrone Street and rummage through the collection. Other designers had the same experience. Bellville Sassoon faced a particularly galling incident during the run-up to the announcement of the engagement. At her mother's suggestion, Diana arrived in the shop looking for a suitable outfit for the announcement, only to be faced by a chief assistant as intimidating as only shopkeepers to the very rich can be. In a scene straight out of *Pretty Woman*, the

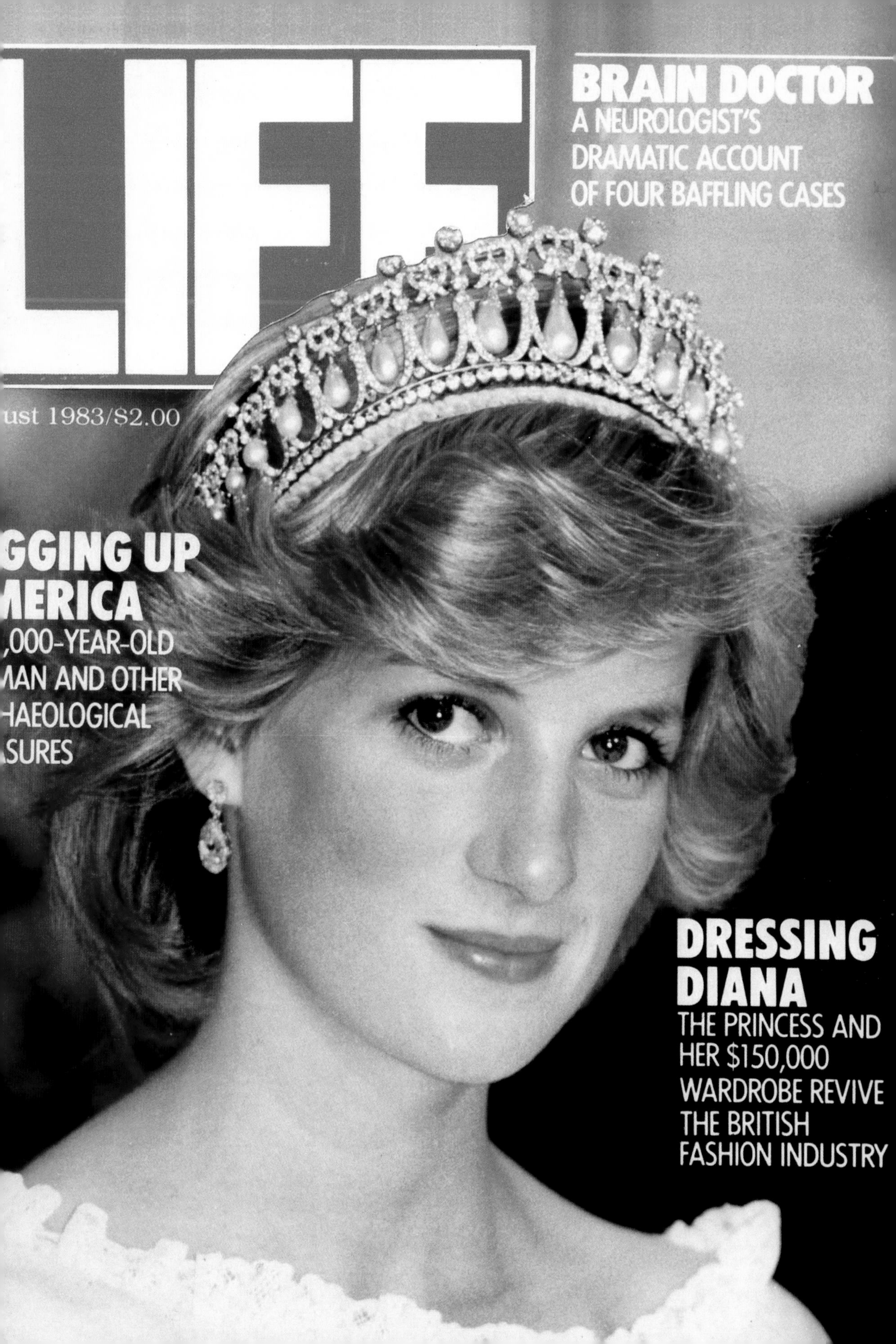
LIFE
ust 1983/$2.00
BRAIN DOCTOR
A NEUROLOGIST'S
DRAMATIC ACCOUNT
OF FOUR BAFFLING CASES
GGING UP
MERICA
,000-YEAR-OLD
MAN AND OTHER
HAEOLOGICAL
SURES
DRESSING
DIANA
THE PRINCESS AND
HER $150,000
WARDROBE REVIVE
THE BRITISH
FASHION INDUSTRY

shop assistant's disdain sent the shy young woman scurrying for the door. Diana headed for the more familiar surroundings of Harrods, where she chose a less-than-flattering blue off-the-peg suit, the hem of which, according to contemporary press rumour, she then unpicked so that she could lower the skirt by two inches. By the time of the official engagement photograph taken with the Queen only days later, some of the damage had been undone. This time Diana posed in a far more successful Bellville Sassoon sailor suit.

After the wedding, all Diana's designers found that there was more formality to the relationship with their most famous customer. Shoemaker Manolo Blahnik recalls, 'The first time Lady Diana visited my shop she came on a bicycle. After the wedding, she came by car, with her driver, and we would empty the shop and close up while she was with us'. The change in the relationship was inevitable, but the princess made it clear that she did not wish it to be so, and even asked all of the designers to carry on calling her Diana. However, even the younger designers, such as Jacques Azagury, Jasper Conran and Bruce Oldfield, with whom Diana would sometimes socialize over lunch, found themselves calling her Ma'am, so conscious were they of the change in her social status. (Margaret Howell remembers instructions coming from *Vogue* to remember to curtsey and call the princess 'Ma'am'.) Like the princess, the designers were determined to treat her new role as her profession. Roland Klein says that he found it so difficult to disobey her injunction to use her first name that he steered conversations to avoid having to call her anything at all.

Nevertheless, the fashion world was one in which Diana could relax and be herself. It is apparent from the stories that the designers tell that Diana soon began to take solace in their company. Suddenly deprived of many of her old friends, or at least of the ability to socialize with them easily, the princess found that the world of London fashion was an easy and rewarding one. Then, as now, it was full of individuals who were witty, gossipy, creative, and above all, fun. They also knew how to be discreet. Seeing all and telling little, society dressmakers need the ability to keep their mouths shut if their businesses are to flourish. As Diana's life within the royal family became more difficult – and later as her marriage began to disintegrate – her clothes provided something of a distraction as well as a means of communication, and the designers became a greater source of support.

It was clear early on to some of the more perceptive among them that the fairytale was not as complete as it might seem. John Boyd recalls, 'To me, she was a poor wee lassie dressing up in her mother's clothes'. Victor Edelstein chose not to try to influence Diana's taste, even though it did not coincide with his: 'She was so pushed around at the palace that I used to feel that I wasn't going to push her around too'.

All of the designers who worked with Diana tell revealing stories about how relaxed she could be. Murray Arbeid recalls how, years later, he used to visit Kensington Palace for fittings. Unlike some other designers, who were less skilled at draping and cutting fabric, Arbeid did not take a fitter with him. His tailoring background – he spent long years working as a cutter before starting his own business – meant that he preferred to do the hands-on work himself. He would be met at the main entrance by a butler and shown into the equerries' room on the ground floor. At a signal from the princess, the butler would escort the couturier up to the drawing room where the fitting would take place. Whenever the princess changed outfits, Arbeid waited in the corridor outside.

On one visit, the young prince William was kicking a ball around and it rolled over to Arbeid's feet. He picked it up and held it out to the young prince who made to grab it. 'What do you say?', said Arbeid, before realizing that he had just reprimanded the heir to the throne. On another occasion, while he was trying to level the bottom of a long red taffeta dress, the prince was playing around beneath the skirts and knocked over a box of pins. At once the princess got down on the floor beside her dressmaker and began helping to pick them up. She recalled a saying from her childhood: 'See a pin and pick it up, and all the day you'll have good luck'. Arbeid made her laugh when he responded with a more cynical version of the rhyme: 'See a pin and pick it up, and all the day you'll have a pin'.

Although increased fame and almost hysterical public adoration made shopping more difficult for Diana, she did still manage to visit some boutiques, usually leaving her driver and bodyguard in the car outside. For instance, a lady-in-waiting would call Roland Klein to make an appointment for the princess to visit first thing in the morning before the boutique was officially open. Klein and his staff did what they could to treat the young woman as she wished to be treated: as an ordinary customer. After she had looked in the store, she would often go into the storeroom to see what extra clothes Klein was making.

On one occasion, she arrived so early that no one was in the storeroom except an assistant, who was doing the washing up. While she waited, the princess happily helped to do the drying. At another time, Roland Klein had a young nephew from France staying who did not understand why his uncle had to be at work so early in the morning. When the reason was explained, he refused to believe it until Klein told the princess the story and asked if he could bring the young boy in to meet her. The nephew's doubt was replaced with tongue-tied nervousness, but the princess soon put him at his ease by chatting to him in French.

Bruce Oldfield recalls how much the princess enjoyed visiting his premises in Fulham. The pair would go into the fabric room and pull out rolls of material that took her interest. They would then carry them up to the office, where they could discuss future plans and the requirements for particular engagements. When Oldfield and his partner Anita Richardson visited Kensington Palace for fittings, they, too, found the atmosphere informal and welcoming. There was always tea and biscuits, and perhaps the young princes playing. Jan Vanvelden, the Dutch-born designer who produced so much of Diana's distinctive daywear, including the famous puritan collars of the early Eighties, enthused at the time, 'She is wonderful to work with because she is interested in what you are doing'.

An occasional presence at some of Diana's fittings with designers was the Prince of Wales. Charles's interest in his wife's appearance is well documented. He once observed, 'You know, I like seeing a lady well dressed. It was one of the things I always noticed about [Diana] before we got married. She had, I thought, a very good sense of style and design'.

After her marriage, the princess would sometimes interrupt a fitting to ask, 'Do you mind if my husband sees this?' Jasper Conran recalls how the prince once came into the room and observed, 'You make the most beautiful clothes for my wife'. When Anna Harvey showed Diana a Murray Arbeid dress at the palace, the princess tried it on and was so pleased that she called her husband. 'I think you look absolutely beautiful', he told his wife. With Bruce Oldfield, the prince pointed at a painting by George Stubbs of an eighteenth-century aristocrat to suggest that the designer might try to emulate the look. It was a re-run of a situation from the Thirties when George VI suggested to Norman Hartnell that he might base the evening dresses for the Queen (later

the Queen Mother) on Winterhalter portraits in the royal collection. Hartnell's creations had been highly successful, and in fact formed the basis for Queen Elizabeth's distinctive style, but Oldfield chose (perhaps wisely) not to pursue the particular direction suggested by Prince Charles.

Rumours soon circulated in the press that Prince Charles was becoming jealous of the attention his wife received. He said that when the couple split up to perform royal 'walkabouts', he always felt that the crowd on his side of the street was rather disappointed, and joked, 'If only I had two wives, to cover both sides of the street'. In New Zealand, he was nonplussed to come face to face with a Di-look-alike competition and observed that none of the contestants 'was as good as the real thing'. But Charles remained deeply interested in his wife's clothes.

One Christmas, the prince telephoned Anna Harvey. He had noticed that his wife did not have an evening coat, and was concerned that she might feel cold when being driven to engagements. Harvey showed him a beautiful Victor Edelstein coat in black velvet lined with white satin, with a fold-down collar. She reassured him that black and white would go over anything. To her surprise, Prince Charles made a very practical protest: 'But it's white. Won't it get dirty?' Gently amused, Harvey told the heir to the throne, 'I could recommend a good dry cleaner'. The prince bought the coat and presented it to his wife, who was thrilled with the present, which she wore in the car on the way to official engagements, taking it off just before she needed to step out in front of the cameras.

In the early years, how Diana managed to keep warm was the subject of great speculation in the tabloids. In December 1983, the *Daily Mail* reported, 'The secret of the Princess of Wales's ability to keep out the cold as she goes walkabout is an undercover job. She's into thermal underwear'. According to the reporter, Diana herself had confessed, 'I am a walking advertisement for Damart'. The paper went on to point out the appropriateness of the revelation: 'Thermal underwear was invented by her great-great-great-great-great uncle, the second Earl Spencer'. A slight overstatement of the facts.

Along with her relaxed informality, Diana won over designers with her great personal charm and her renowned politeness. It was well known that the princess would dutifully write thank-you letters for presents, or following a dinner or other social occasion. Sometimes she would leave an addressed envelope ready on her writing table at Kensington Palace before she went out for the evening so that she could sit down and write a thank-you note as soon as she returned and have it sent first thing in the morning.

It was a habit she had picked up early in her life, and it ran in the Spencer family. After Diana had left for her honeymoon, David Sassoon received a letter from her mother, thanking him for making her daughter look so lovely for her going away. Like other designers, Sassoon also received many letters and cards from the princess, thanking him for particular outfits or noting any compliments. Sassoon says, 'She gave you feedback, so you went to a lot of trouble for her'.

Jasper Conran was another designer who had success with the princess. He, too, was happy to put himself out for her, even if occasionally it made life difficult for his business. Preparing for a sizable royal tour would take over virtually the whole workroom at the same time that Conran was working on his ready-to-wear shows. He jokes that dressing Diana was like running a couture house when he had no intention of running a couture business. Although the princess was happy to buy items from Conran's existing collection, they often required alterations, or she wanted them in different colours.

Diana's designers all discovered that the princess had a feeling for what she wanted, even in the early days. She was very much in charge, and they tried to meet her requirements rather than give her any advice. Bellville Sassoon dressed her for her first Ascot in 1981 in a scarlet sleeveless jacket and a red-and-white candy-striped shirt with puffed sleeves and a pussycat bow. Diana accessorized the outfit with scarlet shoes, white gloves, and a red boater with a scarlet hatband and a large white flower. The whole effect was somewhat overwhelming. Designers, however, found themselves unable to advise the princess to simplify what she was doing. Part of the problem was natural diffidence; Roland Klein recalls, 'I wanted to tell Lady Diana to improve her posture, but I didn't have the guts'.

THE PRINCESS HAD HER OWN DETERMINED IDEAS not simply about fashion but about the nature of sophistication. At times she resembled a small girl let loose in her mother's wardrobe who cannot resist putting on nearly everything at once. What could be more natural for a young woman who had rarely had the chance to express an interest in fashion when she was growing up? Even when she first moved to London, Diana had comparatively little money to spend on clothes. Robina Ziff, who owns the Escada label,

remembers Diana before her engagement coming into the shop and admiring a green evening dress that cost about £450. The young debutante explained, 'I must ask Daddy because it's awfully expensive'.

On the occasions when some of her early outfits may not have been one hundred per cent successful, Diana studied the press criticism in an effort to improve. It was an extremely public learning process, and innumerable unkind things were written about her in the early years. Outfits such as the shocking-pink, low-waisted two-piece she wore to the wedding of her friend Carolyn Pride drew comments that were justifiably negative. To begin with, the suit looked shapeless, the hat was out of proportion to the whole outfit, and the ensemble looked even less impressive when the wind began to play havoc with the long ribbons that dangled from the sailor-suit collar. In 1982, Richard Blackwell, the waspish Los Angeles-based designer and commentator and self-appointed guardian of the Best Dressed lists, went so far as to name the princess as one of the ten worst-dressed women in the world. He compared her to 'a 1910 bathing beauty from a Mack Sennett silent movie' and accused her of rooting in 'Queen Victoria's attic'.

Some experimentation was always going to be necessary to successfully fashion Diana as a modern princess for the media age, and press condemnation was frequently over-harsh. Diana was trying to work out how to transform herself not only into the kind of romantic princess that the public wanted, but also into the formal representative required by the royal family. In addition, of course, she wanted to remain an attractive young wife for her husband. Rarely has one so young and so inexperienced faced such a complex self-transformation in such a glare of publicity. Looking back, Bruce Oldfield believes the answer was simple: 'She needed a stylist. She went off into fashion like a loose cannon – like a kid in a sweetshop. One day a big gown, the next a horrible fussy hat'.

One of the problems was probably the large range of designers that Diana was patronizing at the time. Later, she developed the confidence and knowledge to settle on a smaller handful of reliable partners who would work with her throughout the majority of her royal career. Another was Diana herself: strong, determined to the point of stubbornness, and frequently quixotic, the princess did not like to be told what to do or what to wear. Now her royal status made it even more difficult for designers to influence her. Designers are happiest when a woman puts herself entirely in their hands and makes her body a canvas for their vision. This is why trust is so important in the relationship between couturier and client: the designer must understand precisely the individual he is dressing, while the customer must trust implicitly that the designer will succeed in projecting the image they have of themselves. Not so the princess, still flush with the excitement of the new world of fashion that had suddenly opened up for her. As Jasper Conran observed, 'She needed paring down and simplifying, but there was no chance to tell her'.

Diana's natural instinct to use her clothes as a form of communication – a talent she later mastered to great effect – was already apparent, but in the early years there was none of the refinement and lightness of touch that she later developed. In the words of the American fashion scholar Anne Hollander, 'Her style was extremely conventional. Her clothes at the beginning of her time as princess were faintly ridiculous'. For example, what could be more of a cliché than wearing tartan to Scotland? Yet Diana, in the words of another observer, 'rarely set foot in Scotland without dressing from head to toe in tartan'. John Boyd even made specifically Scottish hats – tam o'shanters or the Scot's soldier's cap called a Glengarry – to go with the outfits. In Wales it was a similar story, with red and green, the colours of the Welsh flag, dominating.

ANOTHER CRITICISM THAT SOON SURFACED about Diana was the extravagance of her clothes shopping. It was rumoured in the press that the princess, bored and bad-tempered during the royal family's holiday in Balmoral in summer 1982, decided to cheer herself up by travelling to London on a whim and spending a fortune on clothes. Such stories dogged Diana for years. It was claimed that she spent $60,000 on clothes every year, while the total value of her wardrobe was estimated to be around $2 million. In 1985, she was widely criticized following unsubstantiated claims that her wardrobe for an official tour to India cost $128,000. However, the princess knew that without new outfits, she could be accused of not making enough effort for the public. She needed new clothes in great quantities. Once, when she asked for a new coat from David Sassoon, he sketched out five for her to choose from; to his amazement, she ordered them all.

Fashion is expensive; good fashion is exceedingly expensive; couture is the most expensive of all. Couture clothes are not intended to be democratic

H.R.H.
PRINCESS OF WALES
H.R.H.
PRINCESS
OF
WALES

or accessible to the majority of women. They are the preserve of an elite that has the leisure and the money to be able to order handmade clothes and lives the kind of high-class social life for which such clothes are appropriate. Diana Spencer crossed into this world when she became engaged to the Prince of Wales, and from that time onward she became not just part of that elite but one of its international leaders.

The type of evening dress in which Diana looked most stunning and that attracted the most positive reaction required many hours of manual work by skilled craftspeople using high-quality materials. One story about the later auction of the princess's dresses for charity in 1997 makes the point well. Roxanne Duke from Maryland bought a cream dinner dress in pleated silk by Catherine Walker for £20,000 and immediately announced her intention to remove about 200 of the fake pearls from the garment so that she could sell them for charity. 'I don't think pulling off 200 pearls will spoil the dress', she said. 'There are thousands on it'. Indeed there were, set as the leaves of flowers with stamens of shimmering glass – and each one of them had to be sewn on individually by the *petites mains* of Walker's studio.

Virtually every one of Diana's evening gowns had a similar level of handcrafted detail: sequins, lacework, diamanté, gilt beads, embroidered stars, a vermicelli effect created by thousands of tiny glass tubes. For an official visit to Saudi Arabia, Walker embroidered the bodice and train of a cream silk dinner dress with falcons made from gold and silver sequins as a compliment to the Saudi royal family. Such quality can never come cheap.

The Princess of Wales's financial relationships with her designers have long been a subject of speculation. It was widely rumoured that the designers donated the clothes without charge; a not entirely philanthropic gesture, given the guaranteed boost to business from being associated with dressing the world's most glamorous woman. It was quite untrue, however. All of Diana's designers billed her in the regular way, although they all offered a discount ranging from 'very big' to 'usual'. A week or two after the bill had been presented, the designer received a cheque in the post. They were always signed by Prince Charles, playing the traditional upper-class role of exchequer for his wife.

In the face of criticism of her spending, the new princess wisely, and not for the first time, took a leaf from the book of her mother-in-law. The Queen has been cleverly adapting and recycling some of her most successful clothes for

decades, asking designers to make small changes here and there to give them new life. After her tour to India in 1985, Diana promised, 'I'm afraid that you're going to see everything time and time again, because it fits, it's comfortable, and it still works'. (In fact, she had already started out that way with the Bellville Sassoon jackets of her going-away outfit. She wore the short-sleeved jacket on her honeymoon, and the long-sleeved one two years later in Australia.)

Diana did make mistakes, but not all of the false starts were the princess's alone. The early Eighties saw a number of British designers lose their way. There was an emphasis on excessive ornamentation that lacked the elegance of designs coming from Paris and New York. Few designers were immune. Bruce Oldfield was criticized for making Diana look glitzy rather than sophisticated or glamorous. In his defence, he argues that he wanted to make the princess sexy rather than romantic: 'the English rose syndrome was never my bag. I liked to see her in much simpler things'.

Oldfield initiated something of a shift in Diana's conventional evening wear in November 1982, when, for a charity fashion show at the Guildhall in London, he dressed her in a dropped-waist, one-shoulder electric blue crepe-de-chine frock reminiscent of the Thirties, with flamboyant Lei-style ruffles around the bodice. Diana complemented the dress with a pearl choker and bracelet. The dress was a departure for a royal princess – it would be difficult to imagine Princess Anne being comfortable in such an outfit at an official function – and showed that Diana was not afraid to innovate.

It also revealed something darker, however: the thinness of the young woman's uncovered arms were the first public sign of the eating disorders that she later sensationally revealed in her TV interview for *Panorama*. Blessed with striking looks, the princess was nevertheless plagued by dreadful insecurity about her appearance. For those who were looking closely, the signs of anorexia were already there, little more than a year into her marriage. But relatively few people were looking closely. Oldfield's extravagance and the romantic optimism of the royal-watching public ensured that it was the elegance of the frock that was remembered rather than the questionable health of the woman wearing it.

She was very influential.

**She put**

and London

**in front of the**

When she was

that

it had an

**London fashion**

designers

**public at large.**

wearing something

was photographed,

mmediate effect.

ROLAND KLEIN

# diana's **hats**

In 1986 Suzy Menkes, writing in *The Times*, credited the princess for the fact that 'Hats are being worn again by the young'. Physically, Diana suited a hat. She had the height and the figure to carry off even large-brimmed creations. What she lacked, though, particularly early in her royal career, was the confidence to wear one. The young Diana was shy and her first hats reflected this. The Lady Di hat created for her by John Boyd, the Scottish milliner, had a distinctive feather but was otherwise as small and discreet as a hat can be.

As she became more confident, Diana began to treat hats as they are most successfully treated: with a sense of humour. There is something faintly absurd in the whole notion of wearing a hat when it is neither cold nor raining, and which would probably offer little protection in either event. New Zealand milliner Philip Somerville convinced Diana to try bigger hats in bolder colours, with contrasting edges or hatbands. There were some uncertain steps as the princess learned what hats went with what outfits and some difficulty in finding exactly the right scale. But ultimately, as Felicity Clark, Diana's early fashion mentor at British *Vogue*, remarks, Diana's big hats were the first sign that she had real chic.

Ironically, given how popular she made hat-wearing among the British middle classes, Diana was not particularly fond of hats, which she associated with formality and protocol. When her press secretary Patrick Jephson once complimented one of her hats as being very 'royal', the princess removed it at once. After her divorce, Diana was no longer obliged to wear hats for social functions, and she stopped doing so virtually altogether. When she did wear hats, she most often chose pillbox styles, which complemented her neat Versace suits. They were a return to the diffidence of her early appearance, as well as a conscious imitation of one of her style heroines, Jackie Kennedy.

'In terms of exports, she is worth millions.'

BRITISH MENSWEAR ASSOCIATION

# a style of her own

WHEN DIANA WORE AN OUTFIT by Bruce Oldfield, the first he had made for her, to switch on the Christmas lights in London's Regent Street in November 1981, the sharp-eyed among the crowds who were not dazzled by the princess's stunning appearance or by the lights themselves might have noticed that she had been unable to fasten the buttons on her navy blue culottes. Diana was pregnant, and already her shape was changing so rapidly that she could no longer button up Oldfield's carefully measured waist.

Victor Edelstein recalls a fitting from the same period: 'The measurements looked strange to me, and the dress was a disaster. I was invited to go to the palace to see if it could be fixed. She put on the dress and it was a monster. We both had to laugh'.

The pregnancy was announced the day after Diana had wowed onlookers with Bellville Sassoon's so-called Gonzaga dress, the frothy and fairytale dress that appealed to the same public who had fallen in love with the romance of the Emanuels' wedding gown.

Diana was feeling anything but a fairytale princess as the stress of her new royal status combined with continual morning sickness took their toll on her health. On her first official visit – Wales was the diplomatic and perhaps obvious choice – the crowds who flocked to see the new princess found her pale and thin, and dressed in the rather predictable red and green of the Welsh

flag. Photographer Jayne Fincher felt some sympathy for her subject: 'She had all these outfits that she turned up in and it just rained nonstop and all the feathers were all bedraggled over her face and all her new coats were soaking and it was really tough going for her. When you're not feeling well, the last thing you want to do is to walk down Carmarthen High Street in a thunderstorm with your new John Boyd hat all ruined'.

News of the pregnancy delighted royal-watchers as much as it dismayed republicans – it was, after all, the constitutional role of the Princess of Wales to perpetuate the royal line. The news seemed even better when the birth of a baby boy, Prince William, on 21 June 1982 guaranteed not only the succession of the throne but also the perpetuation of the house of Windsor. The birth of another prince, Harry, two years later meant that Diana had more than fulfilled her royal obligation. She had delivered what the society pages referred to as 'an heir and a spare'.

Diana later recalled that the six weeks immediately before Harry's birth were the happiest she shared with her husband. When the second baby was not the girl that Prince Charles reportedly wanted, his first comment was apparently 'Oh God, it's a boy', and then, 'and he's even got red hair'. Diana's mother, Frances Shand Kydd, reprimanded the prince for not being grateful simply that the baby was healthy, but by then the damage was done. Diana observed, 'Something inside me closed off'.

FOR BOTH THE PRINCESS AND HER DESIGNERS, motherhood marked a further step in her transition from teenage Sloane Ranger. For Diana, it was another new role: a wife, a princess, now a mother. For most of the people involved in Diana's appearance – by now a team that was beginning to find its feet having been thrust into an unaccustomed role – it was the pregnancy itself that was the major challenge. Anna Harvey readily admits that none of the *Vogue* staff was particularly au fait with, or even interested in, maternity wear. Serious British designers did not do maternity wear, in much the same way as they did not do size 18 or four foot six. It has never figured highly in fashionable clothing. Dressmakers are interested in an ideal body and, failing that, in body shapes that display their clothes to the best advantage, and the feminine form on which they base their vision does not generally come in an antenatal version.

In the early Eighties, the choice of clothes for pregnant women was more or less restricted to tents of billowing floral silk. At the time, the main purpose of maternity wear seemed to be to conceal a woman's bump, and the easiest way to do so was with loose clothes, light fabrics and layers.

Maternity wear did have some adherents, however, and a number of Diana's designers proved adaptable, particularly Roland Klein, who made several dresses for her while she was pregnant. Jasper Conran was another, possibly unexpected, recruit, while Jan Vanvelden's maternity clothes fitted well with his straightforward but feminine daywear.

David Sassoon was initially unwilling to become involved in designing maternity wear for Diana, but the princess was persuasive, and he ended up making a whole collection for her first pregnancy and more dresses for the second. Even so, he confesses, 'Maternity's not my thing. I don't know where to start', and recalls, 'I was never mad on those clothes'. Diana once ordered five maternity coats at the same time – she had learned early the high volume of outfits she would require – throwing Sassoon into a panic. Of the five garments, he now acknowledges, only one turned out to be acceptable.

Sassoon's problem was that he had never produced any maternity wear before. He didn't understand the shapes and found it difficult to make the clothes look right, let alone chic. Even the measurements became a challenge as the princess's stomach grew: virtually every one of the outfits he designed had to be let out. He also had to consider the feel of the clothes for the wearer and how they would appear on camera. Looking back, Sassoon believes that his maternity wear was probably a little on the heavy side for a young woman who felt tired and sick virtually all of the time. (Although morning sickness was not such a problem for Diana when she was pregnant with Prince Harry as it had been with Prince William, it still affected her badly.)

When it came to evening wear, Sassoon was back on firmer ground, however. Diana's broad shoulders and shapely bust allowed his low-cut gowns to focus attention on the top of her body. Even when she was pregnant, the designer recalls, Diana retained her love of feminine and romantic fabrics. On one dress, Sassoon incorporated a piece of lace from Windsor Castle that had once belonged to Queen Victoria. The lace had originally been brought to him by the Duchess of Kent, who wanted to use it to trim a dress. Although Sassoon was reluctant to spoil the lace by cutting it, he did so. At the end of the job, he

found that he had some left over and it was this piece that, unbeknown to the princess, he incorporated into the new gown. He also clothed Diana in a red taffeta empire dress, another intensely feminine look, for the official opening of the Barbican Arts Centre in London on 3 March 1982. For the Braemar Scottish games when the princess was pregnant with Harry, Sassoon followed royal tradition by dressing her in Black Watch tartan, which he again trimmed with romantic lace. Despite his misgivings, Sassoon's maternity wear was some of the most successful that Diana wore.

Victor Edelstein was another designer who was, perhaps unexpectedly, successful at dressing Diana when she was pregnant. Edelstein was an experienced couturier whose stock in trade was the simple but sophisticated, beautiful evening gown. Trained at Alexon, Biba, Salvador and Dior before he started his own company in 1978, Edelstein had a sharp eye for drama, heightened by his interest in designing for the stage. His sense of occasion complemented that of his most important customer.

After Harry's birth, in November 1985, it was Edelstein who provided one of Diana's most noteworthy dresses – memorable not only for its elegance, but also for its theatrical first appearance. Diana was in Washington DC with her husband – *Vogue* reported that her luggage weighed 7,000 pounds – and had packed in her trunks a navy blue velvet column dress by Edelstein. Edelstein had based the bare-shouldered dress and bustle on paintings of Edwardian dinner outfits. When she wore it to the White House for a reception with President and Mrs Reagan, Diana complemented it with a multi-stranded pearl and sapphire choker. The sapphire had originally been given to her by the Queen Mother as a brooch, but Diana disliked brooches generally and found the diamond-encircled sapphire too heavy. She had therefore had the brooch incorporated into a choker by the royal jeweller, Garrard. As the band played 'You're the One That I Want', Diana twirled across the floor with the icon of all disco dancers, John Travolta.

Prince Charles was said to have been upset by his wife's performance. The princess stole the show. To some royal observers, particularly allies of the prince, Diana's antics were a deliberate show of provocation at a time when, behind the scenes, the marriage had begun to break down. It was not the first time. Earlier in the year, Diana had been rebuked by her husband when she made an unannounced appearance on stage, at the Royal Opera House, Covent

Garden, to dance with Wayne Sleep. Diana's friends point out that she had always loved dancing, and continued to take dance lessons and occasionally to join the rehearsals of the London City Ballet. Even so, a dancer as experienced as Sleep knew better than to attempt any serious ballet on that particular august stage. Instead the pair danced to 'Uptown Girl' by Billy Joel, with Diana suitably upmarket and urbane in her silver silk dance dress. The audience called the pair back to the stage eight times, but Prince Charles, up in the royal box where the princess had left him, was aghast. He privately told Diana that her behaviour had been undignified and showy. Again, it was clear that the restrictions of belonging to the royal family were chafing on Diana's essentially independent nature.

MEANWHILE, ANNA HARVEY FROM *VOGUE* had also contacted the Chelsea Design Company, based in Sydney Street in London's Chelsea, which specialized in children's wear and, as a logical extension, in maternity clothing. The company was owned and run by the French-born designer Catherine Walker, who had gone into business five years earlier. Walker was entirely self-taught, having taken up dressmaking as a means of coping with the sudden, premature death of her husband John. Left with two young children to bring up and support, she spent long sleepless nights cutting patterns and learning to understand how the pieces of a garment fitted and worked together. She started out by making rather old-fashioned but lovingly crafted children's angel-tops and pinafores, carrying them in a basket around London clothes stores in order to sell them. Next came maternity wear and the opening of the Chelsea Design Company – Walker jokes that her French compatriots would never allow a new, untrained designer to get away with putting their own name to a business. Her first collection of adult day and evening wear was so successful that Walker had decided to drop maternity wear – until a call came from *Vogue* asking her to make something for the Princess of Wales.

The collaboration thus begun would last until Diana's death. To all intents and purposes, Catherine Walker became Diana's main designer; Diana certainly became her main customer. There were a number of reasons why the two women formed such a close bond. Both came from broken homes, both were naturally shy, and both were trying to feel their way into new roles, one as a princess of the realm, the other as a widow and a businesswoman. Both were somehow outsiders, removed by position or temperament from those around them. But above all, what drew them together was the clothes.

Arguably, Catherine Walker came to understand Diana's needs and what she required from her clothes more successfully than any other designer. And like many of the others, she fell in love with her new customer and was happy to put in the extra effort for her. Walker came to offer the princess what she terms 'total care': she kept permanent spares of cloth in case of some disaster, had staff on standby for emergencies, and even travelled to countries herself to research the specific needs Diana would have on overseas official visits.

In return, Diana acknowledged the closeness of the bond. When she was the guest of honour at the British Fashion Awards in October 1989, she wore a remarkable Catherine Walker white dress embroidered with oyster pearls and sequins with a matching high-collared bolero. (Walker intended the collar design to reflect high-necked Elizabethan collars, but the press crassly dubbed the outfit the 'Elvis dress'). After the ceremony, the princess wrote one of her customary thank-you notes to the designer. It read: 'Dearest Catherine. To my best designer of the year, fondest love from Diana'.

Between them, Anna Harvey believes, Catherine Walker and Diana changed the whole nature of maternity dressing. Rather than try to disguise Diana's condition, they pushed waistlines down beneath her bump, leaving no one in any doubt that the young woman was pregnant – and happy to be so. This was a significant development. It is no exaggeration to claim that it helped to make pregnancy more publicly acceptable; it certainly validated the attempt to remain stylish and visible during pregnancy. The photographs that now fill the pages of celebrity magazines of pregnant stars in low-slung jeans and revealing crop tops would have been absolutely unthinkable thirty years ago. Diana herself could never have gone so far, constrained as she was by royal protocol, and by the prevailing standards of decorum. Nevertheless, it was her two highly visible and highly photographed pregnancies that began the process that made such a seismic shift in social attitudes possible. Perhaps one of the reasons for this was that Diana was a young mother who carried off pregnancy well, certainly in terms of her appearance. She was only twenty years old when she gave birth to Prince William, at a time when the national average for a woman to have her first child was twenty-seven or twenty-eight. Her height helped her body stay in at least some proportion, so that her midriff never came to overwhelm the rest of her.

THE PRINCESS HATED BEING BIG, David Sassoon recalls, and made great efforts to get back into shape after the births of William and Harry. Jasper Conran, too, was impressed by the rapidity with which she regained her figure after the birth of her first baby. Always aware of her body and the need to maintain it, Diana became an almost obsessive exerciser. She would run around Kensington Gardens early in the morning and swim almost every day. She was also a regular visitor to the gym at the Chelsea Harbour Club or elsewhere, where weights routines helped tone her muscles.

Bruce Oldfield says that Diana was essentially 'big-boned and had a big frame'. In Oldfield's sizing, which has always tended to be generous, she varied between a size 10 and a size 12, with a 26- or 27-inch waist. She was tall, too, at five foot ten, with long arms and long legs. Later in their relationship, the designer told the princess that, 'When you're blonde and six foot three in high heels, you could wear a sack and you would still be noticed'. Keeping her body in check was one of the best ways for the young mother to reassert her control of her world.

Married for not quite two years, Diana was trapped in a fairytale that was totally unreal. In private, she was perfectly well aware of the ongoing relationship between her husband and his longtime companion, Camilla Parker-Bowles. As early as the honeymoon, Diana had been upset by Camilla's present to Charles of cufflinks of entwined capital Cs.

Diana also found herself falling out of love with the popular press that had been so supportive during her engagement and for the first eighteen months of her marriage. The royal family was beginning to resent the additional attention that Diana had attracted. The Queen's press secretary, Michael Shea, complained, 'A new wave of royal hysteria has gripped the more sensational press. Anything to do with any aspect of the royal family, no matter how minute, is treated as a news story'.

The royal family had become soap opera, their sagas 'Palace Dallas'. Whether or not the new princess was the prime cause, she was certainly the prime victim. Photographers had begun to tail her everywhere she went, driving at high speed alongside her car to snap her picture. *Time* magazine observed with uncanny prescience in 1983, 'There has been so much of this mad motoring that the wonder is that no member of the royal family or the public has been killed'.

While the princess was pregnant with William, photographers had trailed her and her husband on holiday to the Bahamas, and come away with the most intimate snaps yet. In a clear breach of all royal protocol – and all accepted press protocol at the time – a reporter and photographer set out before dawn to crawl for an hour and a half through hostile terrain to a position half a mile across the sea from the beach where the royal couple was staying. They waited for three hours until, in the middle of the morning, the pregnant princess appeared in a bikini. The reporter was thrilled: 'It was too good to be true'. When the princess proceeded to rub suntan oil into her husband's back it got even better. Just one of the bikini images was rumoured to have been bought by a European magazine for about $35,000.

In Britain, *The Sun* and *Daily Star* both printed pictures of the pregnant Diana – both newspapers insisting that they did so only because of their 'deep affection' for the princess. Each time they explained themselves or apologized, they made sure to publish the offending photographs again. It was the most blatant invasion of privacy Diana had suffered, and it had its effect. From then on she viewed her former allies in the press as potential traitors. Later she would exploit them as tools in her quest to establish her own identity.

Relations with the press worsened further when Diana became the target of vicious stories about the state of her marriage. It was alleged that she had made Prince Charles miserable with her spoiled behaviour and, especially, her relentless shopping, now estimated to cost about $1500 per week. The doyen of gossip columnists, Nigel Dempster of the *Daily Mail*, dubbed her a 'fiend' and a 'monster'; she let down the whole of her class, he claimed, when her alleged temper tantrums drove household staff to resign.

AS THE WINDSOR FAMILY DESCENDED into soap opera – or dangerously close to it in the opinion of constitutional experts as well as journalists – so the clothes in which Diana dressed began to change. They became more showbiz, with shimmering materials and the metallic-effect accessories that she loved, and she wore glossier lipstick and deeper eye make-up. They also became more sophisticated, although Diana remained a long way from the simplified, confident style she later developed. In evening wear, in particular, she began to abandon over-fussy, middle-aged outfits in favour of the less-is-more approach that is the universal signifier of the world's most stylish women. As David Sassoon observes, 'It was only after the birth of Prince Harry that she began to become interested in fashion as opposed to clothes'.

One of the earliest outward signs of this new interest was a subtle change in Diana's shape, as Bruce Oldfield, Catherine Walker and others began to put her in garments that emphasized her broad upper body, often by using shoulder pads and cinched or belted waists above straight skirts or trousers. She was hailed as Disco Di or Dynasty Di – in the current negative climate, some newspapers opted for Di-Nasty.

It was indeed from TV shows that Diana had had the idea of using shoulder pads – Murray Arbeid remembers that she was perfectly capable of arriving at a fitting to declare, 'From now on, only straight skirts', or 'Only wide shoulders'. She was not alone: for huge numbers of middle- and working-class women throughout Britain and the United States, the clothes worn by Joan Collins in *Dallas* and Linda Evans in *Dynasty* epitomized the idea of a classless, urbane chic. Again, Diana's tastes allied her more closely with the millions of ordinary Britons than with the fashion aficionados. It was a theme to be repeated many times. Many years before Tony Blair dubbed her the people's princess in the aftermath of her death, Diana had shown an instinctive ability to communicate with 'ordinary' people though the medium of her appearance.

The factors behind the sudden rise of what was called 'power dressing' in the early Eighties are worth examining. Altering the shape of the body has been a constant in fashion, from the bustles that gave exaggerated curves to Edwardian ladies to the low-slung waistlines and chest-flattening bodices of the flappers to Madonna's pointed bras by Jean-Paul Gaultier. In the early Eighties, too, Japanese designers such as Issey Miyake, Yohji Yamamoto and Rei Kawakubo spearheaded a concerted onslaught on Western fashion from their launching pad in Paris. They used layering and expert cutting to create a series of flat, angled shapes that exerted an almost immediate influence on Western designers. The Japanese themselves reflected the cultural importance of the samurai, using the broad shapes of samurai armour that rose above and squared off the shoulders. Similar shapes had been the prerogative of female power for centuries: the portraits and surviving clothes of Elizabeth I show her determination to echo the broad physical power of her father, Henry VIII, by using padding, ruffs and other devices to make the upper half of the body appear strong.

The man directly responsible for the new popularity of shoulder pads was Nolan Miller, who designed costumes for both *Dallas* and *Dynasty*. Miller had been inspired not by the contemporary world of oil billionaires in Texas, as many people mistakenly assumed, but by sixteenth- and seventeenth-century portraits of powerful women. Actresses such as Joan Collins and, particularly, the broad-shouldered and athletic Linda Evans suited such clothes ideally, filling them with a confident presence. Another former actress also played her part in popularizing the fashion. Nancy Reagan, then the first lady but formerly Nancy Davis the B-movie star, must have been aware from her film career that she had rather a large head in proportion to her body. (Such proportions are common among movie actors, apparently creating a more natural appearance on screen.) As first lady, she used wide-shouldered jackets to bulk out the top half of her body and balance the disproportion.

Women were realizing that they were able to reject the Laura Ashley, soft-focus style of femininity without ignoring their appearance. The philosophical basis of Seventies-style feminism was being abandoned; women were no longer burning their bras or wearing 'genderless' clothes such as dungarees. It was now possible to be very feminine and yet 'masculine' and strong.

The broad shoulders of the new style epitomized this reconsideration of the nature of femininity. The female body was reshaped by fashion into something strong and physical. Meanwhile, thousands of women, like Diana, were entering the traditionally male domain of the gymnasium not only to do their aerobics workouts but also to lift weights and change their body shape. The power dressing of the Eighties was one of the most masculine looks yet to emerge in fashion, yet paradoxically it remained entirely feminine in most cases.

The alteration of the body and the assertion of power were closely associated with the world of business. For a country such as Britain, where the ultra-rich of the United States have always been seen as glamorous, the TV portrayal of Texan oil billionaires and their families was absolutely compelling, and the characters of Alexis and Krystle Carrington became icons of a particular type of strong, self-assertive woman. It was perhaps this element of the new silhouette that the Princess of Wales admired. What could be more appealing to a naturally shy woman with rounded shoulders than clothes that almost literally protected her with a covering that echoed the archetypal inverted-V shape of power, that of the shield? Again, Diana was in the vanguard, changing her shape not only through her clothes but also through exercise. Later in life, when her body had become even more toned and shaped, she was able to abandon any artifice in her clothes and wear the simplest of shift or wrap dresses, letting her body make its own impression.

ONE OF HER CHIEF ALLIES in the change of silhouette, Bruce Oldfield, had become something of a professional and personal favourite of the princess. Like other designers in the early period, Oldfield recalls that Diana was not yet the ideal fashion plate she later became. She had a tendency to hunch her shoulders and duck her head, which it is easy to put down to her natural shyness as well as her self-consciousness about her height. She also had a way of locking her knees so that they bent backward, pushing her hips forward and ruining the line of straight skirts by opening the back vent. Oldfield – who at the time was the only designer dressing the princess in straight skirts – recalls lecturing his client about her posture during fittings. 'You'll thank me when you're older', he told her.

The former Barnardos boy made fifty or sixty outfits for the Princess of Wales; with his natural charm, he also became a regular companion for lunch at Diana's favourite hangouts. Typical of Oldfield's more dramatic silhouettes – what Jasper Conran calls 'cookie cutter clothes' or 'cardboard cutouts' – was a wide-shouldered, long, red crepe dress with a dramatic slit down the back. Diana wore it to the first Birthright Ball at the Albert Hall in 1984.

The relationship between the princess and the designer was not always easy for Oldfield. The clothes in his collection often had to be heavily adapted for Diana's particular needs. And he felt that he did not get on particularly well with Anna Harvey, which made the relationship with the princess constantly insecure. The payoff, however, was perhaps even greater for Oldfield than for any of Diana's other designers, with the possible exception of the Emanuels. In the early part of the Eighties, Oldfield was not necessarily the best designer in London but he was without doubt the most famous. In newspapers and Sunday magazines, on *Wogan* and other TV chat shows, Bruce Oldfield was the face of a certain type of British fashion. That he had risen from an orphanage to rub shoulders with the likes of the Princess of Wales made his story almost as romantic as was Diana's. The pair were natural allies throughout virtually all of the decade, until the princess quite suddenly stopped using him around 1989.

The high point of their relationship came in 1985, when Diana was Oldfield's 'date' for a charity dinner on behalf of Barnardos, of which she was the president. By then, Diana had long abandoned the royal protocol of wearing gloves but she still carried an evening bag, usually a small clasp one. Oldfield used to tease her because 'She never had to carry anything!' At the ball at the Grosvenor House Hotel, however, when the princess wore an Oldfield dress of Fortuny-pleated metallic lamé, she opened her clasp bag to reveal that it contained just one item: a packet of cigarettes she had thoughtfully brought for the heavy-smoking designer.

ANOTHER NEW ALLY IN DIANA'S evolving appearance was Philip Somerville, who was probably her most successful milliner. The small, feathered hats from her mother's milliner, John Boyd, had been left far behind, although the style will be known forever as *the* Princess Diana hat. Diana began to broaden her tastes, working with more talented milliners such as Freddie Fox and Graham Smith, who had a more chic sense of combining a hat with an outfit.

After seeing one of Somerville's hats on TV, Diana asked her current hairdresser, Richard Dalton, to make enquiries about the designer. A few phone calls later, princess and hairdresser turned up at Somerville's boutique. Urbane New Zealander Somerville had worked in London for years, decorating the heads of the social elite, including the Queen and other members of the royal family, and was lucky to come into contact with Diana at the start of what he calls her 'grown-up period'. No longer would the princess be seen in fussy feathers or bows: she was coming to realize that less is more. Somerville achieved much in the eleven years he worked with his customer, but he pithily sums up his essential contribution: 'I was the guy who put the princess into big hats'.

Somerville gave Diana larger brims, sometimes with contrasting edges or hatbands, which protected her from the sun in hot countries but also left her face clearly on show. The hats were elegant but not without playfulness; for example, for a hat for an official visit to Bangkok, Somerville styled the crown in a point to echo a pagoda. On another occasion, when Diana was visiting Japan, he put a rising sun on a hat, which amused the emperor. Predictably, fashion purists were appalled.

Designing successful hats is all about scale, and in that respect making hats for Diana could be quite difficult. She had, Somerville recalls, a large head:

Diana used to remark, 'Of course it won't fit me; my head's too big'. The first hats the princess tried on were inevitably all too small; they simply sat on the top of her head. Only after Somerville had made a wooden block to the size of Diana's head was he able to create samples that gave a true impression of how the hats might eventually look.

From 1986 until the end of Diana's life, Philip Somerville made nearly all of her hats for official engagements – although she virtually stopped wearing hats altogether after her divorce in 1996, seeing them as part of her royal 'uniform' rather than as an expression of her personality. Just as Catherine Walker had become Diana's dressmaker, so Somerville became Diana's milliner. The pair had to work in close coordination. Walker would sometimes send sketches, or even the outfits themselves, for Somerville to study. She would also send fabric so that the hat would be sure to match the dress, something that had not always happened successfully in Diana's earlier career. For each outfit, Somerville would mock up four or five possible shapes from which Diana would select, usually at fitting sessions at Kensington Palace.

Somerville kept some characteristics of Diana's earlier headwear, such as the small veils that gave her something to hide behind. In his wide brims, however, he was an innovator, and with some particular designs he bordered on the tricksy. For a visit to Abu Dhabi in 1989, he put a blue quill and a white brim on top of a blue turban that wrapped around the princess's head and over her ears, trying to observe local custom of modesty for women. He recalled that the press hailed the hat as a remarkable breakthrough. Somerville commented 'We had thought of it to cover up her hair'. To complement an Escada yellow and black coat, Somerville again made a turbanlike shape in matching colours, although he professes not to be keen on the hat.

DIANA'S EFFECT WAS SPREADING THROUGHOUT the royal family. The Queen herself adopted shoulder pads in April 1986, in a buttercup yellow coat by Ken Fleetwood at Hardy Amies, which marked a distinctive change in her silhouette. It might have been no coincidence that Diana herself had become a customer of the august royal couture house. Only Prince Charles seemed immune. Although his wife was given credit for improving his choice of shirts, the British Menswear Association complained in 1985, 'It is not that he actually dresses badly; it is that his clothes are dull, boring and much too safe. The last

Prince of Wales (who became King Edward VIII) was a real trendsetter and had as much influence on men's fashions in his day as Princess Diana does on women's today. In terms of exports, she is worth millions'.

Shoulder pads were, like the soap operas that inspired them, a passing phenomenon. It was their great apostle, Oldfield himself, who signalled the change in October 1986, when he dressed Diana for the British Fashion Banquet at Fishmongers Hall in London in an off-the-shoulder dress that looked back to the Renaissance. For customers who were nervous about abandoning their broad shoulders, Oldfield offered the dress with a mink trim, but Diana diplomatically chose to do without. *The Times* noted perceptively that when Diana sat beneath a portrait of the young Queen Victoria, the two dresses were strikingly similar. The modern princess was unconsciously returning to more royal forms of dress.

A number of designers found themselves in potentially awkward situations with members of the royal family who were eager to follow Diana's lead even to the extent of outright imitation. When one of the royal duchesses visited Roland Klein's boutique, she would always ask, 'Has the Princess of Wales been in?', meaning that she wanted to copy Diana's wardrobe. It was easier, the designer decided, simply to instruct the shop assistants to tell the customer that they did not know. Designers are suitably discreet about naming names, of course, but they make it clear that the diplomacy of royal dressing did create some tensions between them and some of the royal duchesses.

Diana, they widely agree, was not exclusive. She laid down no edicts about whom designers could or could not dress. She did not demand that clothes be made only for her. She was, by and large, happy to choose garments from the designers' prepared collections, and would simply specify different colours or other small variations. There was always the risk, however, that sooner or later she might be confronted by someone wearing virtually the same outfit.

It nearly happened at least once. Murray Arbeid made Diana a strapless tulle gown in navy with little diamanté stars and a very full skirt. He made the same dress for Queen Noor of Jordan. After a birthday party at Claridges the designer received an angry letter from Queen Noor pointing out that had she not decided to change at the last moment, both women would have been wearing exactly the same outfit. However, as Arbeid explains, in a ready-to-wear business, he sells a number of every dress design, including this one. Complete exclusivity inevitably costs more.

It's a situation that has occurred before: a limited number of society dressmakers clothing a limited social group makes it unavoidable. Jan Vanvelden dressed Diana as well as Princess Michael and the Duchess of Kent; Bellville Sassoon included Princess Margaret in its list of customers, again with the Duchess of Kent; the Emanuels made clothes for the Duchess of Kent and for the Duchess of York; Alistair Blair dressed both Fergie and Diana.

When two of Hartnell's customers found themselves at a function in exactly the same clothes, they did what most women would do in such a potentially embarrassing situation: they laughed uproariously and carried it off with great aplomb. The next day, however, the couturier received a letter from one of them complaining that she had never been so insulted in her life. Such are the dangers of dressing Britain's social elite. It has been the same at courts throughout history. In gatherings where every detail and nuance of dress carries implications about rank and status, the dressmaker is dragged into a world of finely balanced judgements, not all of which he or she gets right.

EARLY IN 1986, THERE WAS SPECULATION about how much advice Diana would be able to offer the latest addition to the royal family: her friend Sarah Ferguson was about to marry Prince Andrew. The press was beside itself with excitement.

Sarah Ferguson – quickly dubbed Fergie in the popular press – was everything Diana had not been. She was confident, outgoing, a woman of the world. She had held down a steady job in publishing, unlike the Princess of Wales, who had only nannied and looked after young children. Sarah Ferguson was loud, brassy and comfortable with her fuller figure. She had a sense of fun that would later get her into trouble when it appeared that she did not take her royal duties quite as seriously as she might. She was a self-confessed tomboy who was perhaps more at home in everyday wear than her more graceful friend.

The two women had been friends for years, however. Diana had met Sarah soon after starting to date Prince Charles. Whenever Diana went to watch her fiancé play polo, Sarah would be there also, as the daughter of Charles's polo manager, Major Ronald Ferguson.

The British press instantly began a predictable campaign to compare the two young women's wardrobes. Diana, it must be said, had something of a head start: she had become accustomed both to life in the limelight and to

killy
ROSSIGNOL
Raichle

dressing for the occasion. But Fergie was not entirely innocent of such matters – she had been photographed with Diana many times in the early Eighties as they enjoyed watching polo and at other social occasions. It seemed obvious that Sarah Ferguson would follow Diana's lead.

To some extent, that is exactly what she did, though not quite as completely as many people had predicted. The change was clear from the very start when, for the official engagement announcement in March 1986, she commissioned the rising young designer Alistair Blair. Having trained at Dior and Givenchy, and worked as Karl Lagerfeld's assistant at Chloe, Blair had only just started his own label, with the powerful backing of the entrepreneur Peder Bertelsen. The commission from Sarah Ferguson came at just the right time to help get the business off the ground.

With only twenty-four hours to come up with an outfit, Blair created a short, boxy double-breasted wool jacket with a black leather belt over a long skirt that fell to the middle of the calf. The silhouette was both new and self-consciously old fashioned, harking back to the shapes of the Forties and Fifties. Blair carried over his fascination with older styles to evening wear when he dressed the Duchess of York, as Sarah became, in dramatically large evening dresses with bustles and inflated skirts. Like Diana, Sarah Ferguson made a number of successful relationships with designers, of which the one with Blair was one of the most productive.

Some of Diana's designers also initially worked for the duchess, including Catherine Walker. Other designers, however, tell stories of how they were discouraged – directly or indirectly – from dressing other royals in addition to the princess. For some, it was a question of loyalty: they had dressed the princess for years, and in every case had benefited greatly from the exposure they received when she wore their clothes. They enjoyed working with her and being with her, with her ready sense of fun and her polite appreciation and thoughtful notes. She was 'their' princess just as they were 'her' designers. If they had to make a choice between the two royal customers, there would be no contest.

Bellville Sassoon dressed Fergie, as did many of Diana's other designers, particularly early on in her royal career. But the Duchess of York tried to find her own fashion path, probably realizing that it was unrealistic to compete with Diana apart from on her own terms. For her wedding dress, for example, she turned to a virtually unknown designer, Lindka Cierach. Of Polish and English extraction, Cierach had been born and brought up in Africa before being educated in England. She worked at *Vogue* before studying at the London College of Fashion, after which she soon began working on her own. *Tatler* had spotted her and predicted that she would become the 'hottest society dressmaker' just months before Sarah Ferguson commissioned the wedding dress.

The dress could barely help but be influenced by the Emanuels' fairytale dress for Diana. Cierach again went for ivory silk duchess satin with a fitted bodice that fell to beneath the waist. She avoided the problems with creasing that had bedevilled the Emanuels' dress by making the front of the skirt flat. Whereas Diana had had a twenty-five-foot train, Sarah's was only seventeen and a half feet. But these are minor details: the fact is that when Sarah Ferguson walked down the aisle on 23 July 1986, everyone watching judged the wedding by comparing it to *the* royal wedding five years earlier. Although this second wedding was free of much of the protocol attached to marrying the heir to the throne, it was essentially the royal wedding on a smaller scale. Inevitably perhaps, there was a feeling that Sarah Ferguson was a poor substitute – Diana-lite.

As if to make her own mark, Sarah Ferguson at once began to patronize designers that Diana had never used, in particular the established French house of Yves Saint Laurent. She also continued the bold experimentation with shape that she had started with Alistair Blair and his carefully structured clothes. Many of her outfits continued to have a conscious echo of the Forties and Fifties, such as the full-skirted, polka-dot taffeta ball gown YSL made for the 1987 Leukaemia League of 365 ball, which was hosted by Joan Collins at London's Café Royal. Zandra Rhodes was another designer whose somewhat erratic way with colour had not suited the Princess of Wales, but whose style fitted better with the Duchess of York's larger-than-life personality.

The duchess, the papers agreed, was a breath of fresh air in the royal family: a woman who looked as if she could have fun. Diana seemed reserved by comparison – and for good reason. Not only were their personalities different, but she was not as free to be herself as Sarah Ferguson was, in the same way that her husband had never been as free as his younger brother.

Fergie certainly had her own appeal to the public. She too became something of an unlikely fashion leader. Her favourite fabric, double duchess satin, was used extensively by Blair and others for formal clothes, and was so widely imitated that suppliers in England and France had difficulty keeping

up with demand. The tightly fitted jackets, with trademark bows often sewn at the small of the back, also became highly fashionable, as did bustle-back suits. The elements of humour Fergie introduced into her wardrobe – a dress printed with teddy bears in a reference to her love for the toys, or a small Chanel Christmas tree brooch worn to a carol concert – were new to the royal family and many observers found them refreshing. But the duchess's fashion sense often lacked the sureness of touch that her sister-in-law had by now developed. One particular outfit, designed by Alistair Blair for Fergie's meeting with the Red Arrows – was a fitted red suit accompanied by red darts in Fergie's red hair and worn with a black and white roll-necked satin blouse. The overall effect as the duchess strode across the tarmac with the pilots was of an air hostess trying to find the right plane.

Diana's initial response, somewhat unwisely, was to try to act more like Fergie. Such was the pressure upon her that she thought that was what people wanted. When the press praised Fergie as a breath of fresh air, Diana said, 'I was listening and reading every line. I felt terribly insecure'. And unfortunately the press wasn't the only problem: Prince Charles apparently once asked her 'Why can't you be more like her?'

Diana tried: she turned up with Fergie and comedienne Pamela Stephenson in police uniform to crash Prince Andrew's stag night in a central London club. She went to a David Bowie concert with other young royals and wore what she thought people wore to such occasions: leather trousers. 'I completely put out of my mind that I was the future Queen and future queens don't wear leather like that in public. Slapped hands.'

For a while, relations between the two royal women became strained: 'I got terribly jealous and she got terribly jealous of me', recalled the princess. As Fergie ran out of energy, or perhaps enthusiasm, for coping with the demands of royalty, however, the pair grew close again. She repeatedly asked Diana, 'How have you coped with this for all these years?'

The answer, we now know, is 'with difficulty'.

The press were in love

**she looked**

she sold

**no one could**

with Diana …

**terrific,**

magazine covers,

**get enough of her.**

ROY GREENSLADE

# diana's **jewellery**

Britain's royal jewels are among the most outstanding in the world, and over the course of her royal career, Diana, like her mother-in-law, Queen Elizabeth II, accumulated one of the world's greatest collections of jewellery. She had pieces ranging from priceless sapphires and family heirlooms to pearls and shiny costume jewellery. But Diana did not simply amass jewellery, she experimented with it; she adapted her Queen Mary choker as a headband, and once wore a necklace of pearls trailing down behind her backless dress and tied in a small knot.

At the outset, Diana had little jewellery – she borrowed pieces from respected jewellers during her engagement – but as wedding presents she received breathtaking jewels from around the world, particularly a sapphire diamond suite from Saudi Arabia.

One of Diana's favourite pieces was her engagement ring of sapphire surrounded by eighteen diamonds; Charles and Diana chose it from a selection of eight sent around to the palace by Garrard, the royal jeweller. It was immediately widely copied, though generally on a far more modest scale.

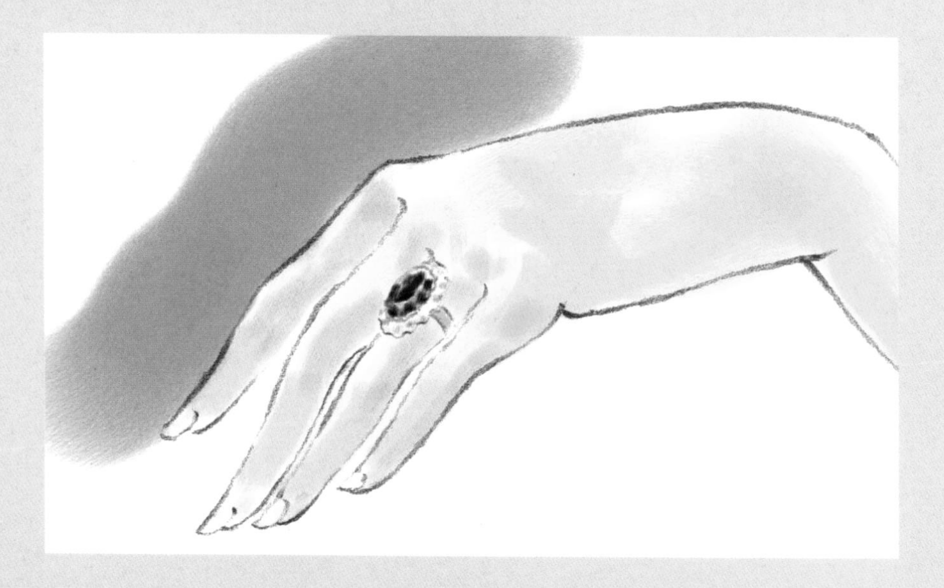

Diana was guided in her choice of jewellery by two of Britain's most respected jewellers, Collingwood and Garrard. Edward Green, who worked at both, advised the princess throughout her career and was able to help with storage (no small consideration with a collection said to be worth about £27 million pounds in total) and with remaking or redesigning jewels Diana wanted to change. For example, as an engagement present, the Queen Mother gave her a brooch consisting of a large sapphire surrounded with diamonds. After a few outings, Diana had the sapphire mounted on a seven-string pearl choker that became her signature style.

Diana's most famous single piece of jewellery was the Spencer tiara, a family heirloom, which she wore for her wedding, although it was unfortunately somewhat lost in her hair. The tiara is made of gold and silver scrolls and foliage, with stars and tulips, and decorated with diamonds. Despite its antique appearance (family legend had it that it dated from the 1760s), it was apparently made around the middle of the nineteenth century, although the two small scrolls at either end remain from an earlier setting.

'She'd changed her look, found a stylist and a hair stylist... and gained a new kind of confidence.'

PATRICK DEMARCHELIER

# international **stage**

EARLY IN 1992, DURING A royal tour of India, Prince Charles was engaged to address a meeting of businessmen. It was the essence of his royal role, representing British interests overseas. Unbeknown to him, only a few miles away, his wife was using all her media and fashion savvy to make a devastating but unspoken comment on the state of their marriage. Few displays of public misery have spoken more clearly than Diana's solo trip to the Taj Mahal, the monument built by the heartbroken Mughal emperor Shah Jahan to his dead wife.

In the decade since taking on her new role as Princess of Wales, Diana Spencer had come a long way – in the way she presented herself to the world, in her understanding of her relationship with the camera and in her unerring ability to create iconic images. The clothes Diana chose to wear were secondary to the carefully stage-managed scene – sitting alone on a stone bench in front of the beautiful love-letter in stone – but they were significant. The princess wore a bold bolero suit of flaming red, violet and yellow by Catherine Walker, the designer in whose clothes she felt most at home. The outfit was both exotic in its colours and utterly practical in its cool silks, but above all, it was as defiant and strong as the traditional dress of India itself.

As if to underline the poignancy of her situation, Diana had recycled the outfit: Walker had originally designed the suit for an official visit to Hong Kong three years earlier. There, Diana had worn it with Philip Somerville's

witty 'pagoda' hat in matching violet and red to give an appearance of perky confidence. On this occasion, she abandoned headwear altogether. As she sat with her head bowed slightly forward, as if in contemplation of her unfortunate circumstances, she was surely well aware that royal-watchers worldwide would get the message.

It was a bad moment for Prince Charles. His wife had become one of the great silent communicators of the modern mass-media age, as well as one of the most photographed and commented upon women in the world. Now, at the most strained time in their marriage, she had dealt him what royal-lovers would see as a sneaky and underhand blow by posing as if she were entirely alone, and wearing what, in royal circles, were old clothes. It seemed inevitable: if there was to be a villain in the affair, Diana at least was determined that it would be her husband. For that reason, she was to pose, albeit briefly, as the victim, almost as if in rehearsal for the infamous Martin Bashir TV interview.

That role was cemented in June, with the publication of *Diana: Her True Story*, a book in which the princess was widely known to have cooperated with journalist Andrew Morton. The book detailed her depression, the fragile state of the royal marriage, Diana's struggles with eating disorders and her strained dealings with many of her royal relations. Shortly afterward, things grew worse when press reports of an intercepted telephone call revealed a romantic relationship between Diana and James Gilbey, only the first in a string of reputed lovers of the princess.

The reaction among royal-watchers varied from outrage at this public airing of the dirty laundry of the royal family to anxiety about the very fabric of the British constitution as well as concern for Diana's welfare. And, of course, there was a large dose of mild scepticism among republicans. At the heart of the story, however, there remained an individual in emotional distress. Diana was far from the uncertain, shy teenager who had married her prince charming, but she still lacked the resources to be able to face such a crisis alone. There was still, at the heart of her, a vulnerability that seemed highly at odds with the confident persona projected by her appearance.

The British people largely appreciated this contradiction between the public and private faces, and they understood the burden it placed on the princess. Sympathy for her grew – in hindsight perhaps a little too much, as Diana herself was not entirely passive in her estrangement from her husband.

The publication of the Morton book, like the photo session at the Taj Mahal, reflected just how much she was prepared to manipulate the attention of the media to put across her side of the story. In the eyes of the people, however, the princess remained virtually untarnished.

DIANA'S REACTION TO THE PROBLEMS she faced was to throw herself into her work. She was still a member of the royal family, she still fulfilled official engagements on behalf of the British crown, she was still the patron of many charities. In Diana's own mind, her role was very simple. As she sentimentally but possibly correctly expressed it: 'I knew what my job was, it was to go out and meet the people and love them...'

She also, crucially, returned to silence, for now at least. Having spoken out to Morton and made her case – and aroused the fury of much of the media – Diana left it to her appearance to communicate with the masses. It was for her ability to suggest a whole world of suffering inside her, or a whole well of compassion for others, that the American feminist Camille Paglia astutely identified Diana as the last of the silent movie stars. She did not need words to fight her battles. The fiercely intellectual Paglia was an unlikely ally for a woman with, to all intents and purposes, no academic training, who set more store by passion than by thought, but her assessment was accurate.

By keeping her counsel while looking great, Diana managed to emerge from the year with her reputation largely intact, even after the unsurprising announcement on 9 December 1992 that the royal couple were separating. In March 1993, when *OK!* was launched as a new celebrity weekly in Britain, there was only one choice for the cover star: the princess. Anne Wallace, the editor who made the choice, remarked, 'Diana is still very popular. There are certain celebrities who divide readers, but you could put Diana on anything, even a baked bean tin'. In a cut-throat world where, according to the British media company IPC, the right cover is calculated to add about twenty per cent to magazine sales, the testament to the princess's continued pulling power was clear.

Diana moved from Highgrove House in Gloucestershire and permanently back into her quarters in apartments No. 8 and 9 in Kensington Palace, defying Prince Philip's suggestion that she give them up to allow Prince Charles to keep them on as his London base. She took with her Paul Burrell as her personal butler, and set about gathering around her a staff whose loyalty could not be questioned. She spent more time with her closest friends, including Lucia Flecha de Lima, Rosa Monckton and Lady Annabel Goldsmith, or the Duchess of York, regularly meeting them for lunch at the palace or at nearby restaurants such as Launceston Place or San Lorenzo.

For the most recognizable woman on the planet, however, life in Kensington Palace – Diana invariably referred to it as KP – was often rather empty, particularly in the evenings when most of the staff had gone home, or when the two princes were away at boarding school. A number of times, Burrell admitted in his autobiography, princess and butler would settle down in the evening to watch a DVD together, before he was able to slip away and return to his own family home.

Diana sought consolation for her troubles in a whole range of well-publicized ways, including more trips to the gym. Some designers, such as Bruce Oldfield and Jacques Azagury, felt that the physical changes resulting from all these workouts were not all beneficial, that the wider shoulders and bigger upper arms made the princess look a little less feminine. Roland Klein agrees: 'At one point I think it became too much'. For most people, however, Diana continued to be an inspirational figurehead: she proved that anyone could change things about themselves they might not like – especially the shape of their body.

More consolation came from the widely talked about – and widely derided – colonic irrigation, which promised benefits of purging the system and losing a few pounds. It may or may not work, but Diana's adoption of it was a clear sign of her willingness to consider unconventional therapies and medicines. This attraction to the alternative was increasingly in evidence as she became more her own person – and in this respect, at least, she had something in common with her estranged husband. In his day, Charles himself had been lampooned for his interest in organic farming, talking to plants and taking spiritual advice from all manner of seers and sages.

Rather like her stepmother's mother, Barbara Cartland, Diana believed in natural therapies and homeopathic remedies. She summoned masseurs and fitness trainers to the palace and began to consult an endless series of astrologers, psychotherapists and self-help experts. Inevitably, perhaps, the princess was sometimes accused of credulity for her willingness to listen to such unqualified 'experts' – 'My astrologer tells me my husband will never be

nov. 10th 1993.

king', she told her press secretary in June 1992. But all of Diana's experimentation can be seen in another way: as a continual search for the self-confidence that would help close the gap between her character and her appearance so that she could live up to her own iconic image.

DRESS CONTINUED TO BE AT THE HEART of Diana's life. At Kensington Palace, she had an L-shaped room to contain what was by now a huge wardrobe of clothes, where rails of colour-sorted dresses and jackets hung above hundreds of pairs of shoes, all of which were carefully coordinated with the clothes immediately above them. Clothes and shoes were all hidden away behind protective curtains that lined the dressing room. It was here each morning that Diana sat in her white robe while she decided on the outfit for the day. In this, at least, she had more freedom than before.

As the tensions within the royal marriage had worsened, butler Paul Burrell had witnessed how clothes had become a battleground between husband and wife. In Japan in November 1990, the princess, wearing a red tartan coat dress by Catherine Walker, with collar and cuffs in red velvet, had made her way down a staircase toward the rest of the waiting royal party ready to leave for an official function. The outfit was certainly bright enough to gain attention – as all of Diana's clothes needed to be – but did not quite justify Charles's apparent reply when the princess asked him 'Do you like my outfit, Charles?' The prince replied, 'You look like a British Caledonian air stewardess'.

A few months later, in Prague – by which time the royal couple were staying in different rooms, and in fact on different floors – the princess put on an off-white suit with black buttons and a black handkerchief in the breast pocket. Unbidden, the prince's observation this time was allegedly, 'You look like you've just joined the mafia'.

Fashion is often a game of judgement, and the line between success and failure can be very thin. With an unanticipated gust of wind or an unwise choice of accessories, what might begin as an elegant and flattering outfit can cause great embarrassment and turn its wearer into a laughing stock. One suit that drew particular criticism was worn by Diana in 1987 when she met King Fahd of Saudi Arabia at Gatwick Airport. Designed by Catherine Walker, the ivory suit had elaborate frogging of gold braid across the front, echoed on the back, the whole topped off with a heavy hat.

Rather than decry Britain's political involvement with the autocratic and deeply questionable Saudi regime, the press decided to attack the princess's dress sense. She looked, one newspaper said, like a drum majorette. Another commented that she resembled one of the cardboard cut-outs of the Beatles on the front of the 'Sergeant Pepper' album cover. Both comments were entirely justified in the opinion of sophisticated fashion-followers, many of whom felt that Catherine Walker's lack of training through either college or an apprenticeship had let down the princess.

The chances of making a fashion faux pas are always increased by the addition of headwear. In the opinion of milliner Stephen Jones, who made berets for the princess late in her royal career, a hat can turn an outfit into costume only too easily. As he says, 'It adds drama, status and theatricality, and the person behaves a little differently'. When clothes become costume, the threat of pantomime is never far away. The high pillbox hat made by Graham Smith at Kangol, who reportedly had to hand stitch it overnight to get it finished on time, undoubtedly contributed to the marching-band look of the ensemble. The mystery is that Diana, by now quite fashion savvy, seemed to view her role as dressing as if playing a pantomime role. For one who paid so much attention to what was written about her clothes, Diana could react stubbornly to criticism and, in this case, persisted with the error: she wore the outfit again shortly afterward. This time, the occasion had real military overtones: she was visiting army cadets at Sandhurst.

AFTER HER SEPARATION FROM PRINCE CHARLES and her move back to Kensington Palace, Diana's choice of clothes for the day was, as always, dictated by what she had to do. For visits to hospitals, for example, and particularly to children's hospitals, she would wear something brightly coloured to try to cheer up the patients. One particular favourite was a paintbox silk dress by David Sassoon in dark blue patterned with brightly coloured abstract flowers in turquoise, yellow and red. Diana called it her 'caring dress', and after it was made in 1990, she wore it many times. So many times, Sassoon remembers, that one paper printed an article saying that the princess should throw it away.

The colourful dress had short sleeves because, Diana explained, she liked to touch people: 'Yes, I do touch. I believe that everyone needs to be touched'.

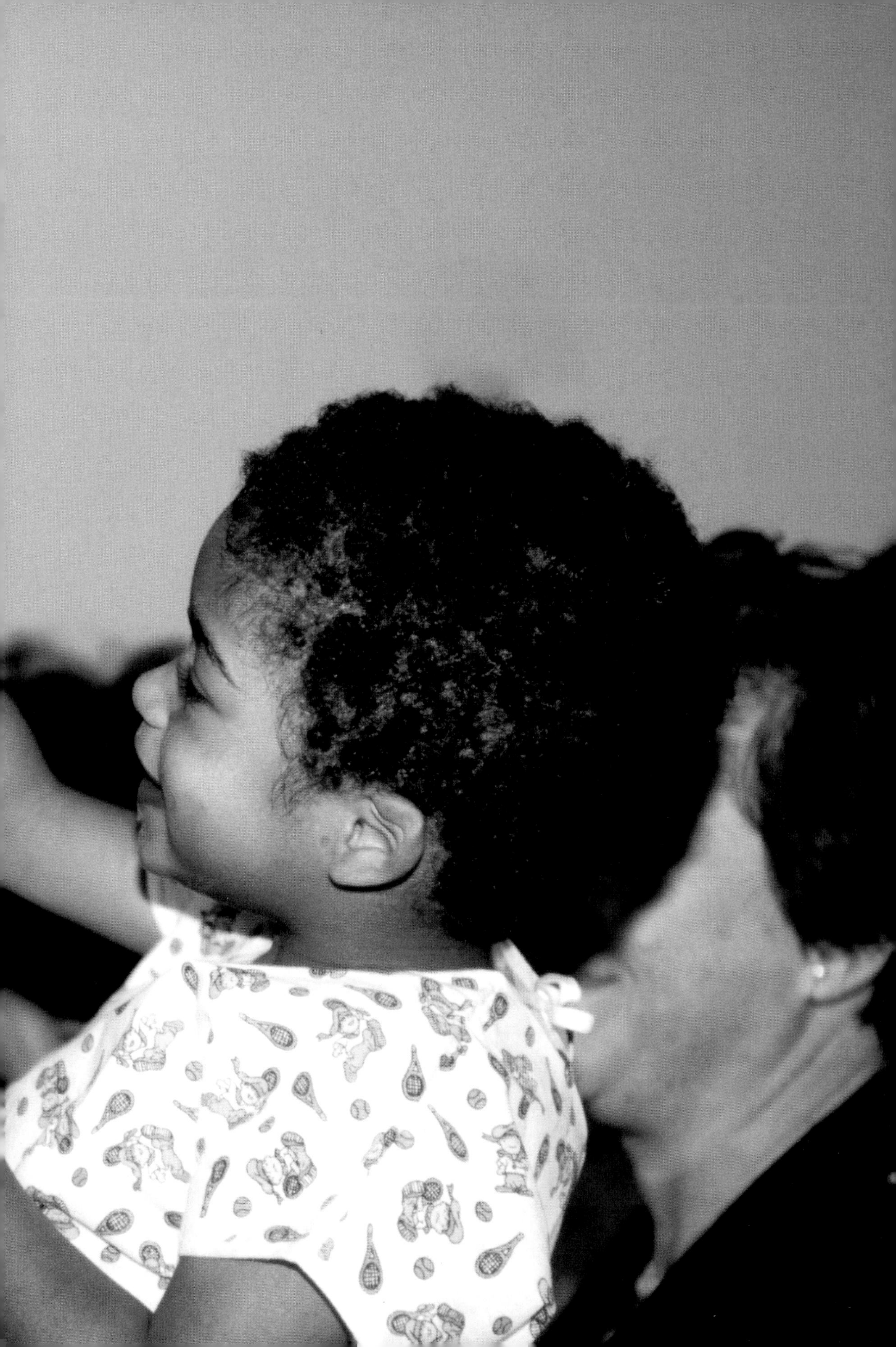

(She had abandoned the royal protocol of wearing gloves at formal occasions for the same reason.) In 1987, she had famously allowed herself to be photographed shaking hands with an HIV/AIDS victim in a London hospital, to help discourage the idea that the disease was contagious. In 1991, she wore the 'caring' dress in Brazil, where she cuddled babies who had been born HIV positive. If she was visiting the blind, the princess was always careful to wear clothes with an interesting texture, so that the people she spoke to would be able to feel her presence. For children, she wore dangling necklaces and made sure that neither her jewellery nor her buttons would scratch them.

For her continuing programme of public duties, Diana further refined her choice of dressmakers. Catherine Walker remained a constant, as did Murray Arbeid. There were some casualties, however. Anna Harvey at *Vogue*, who remained Diana's closest fashion adviser throughout her life, recalls that some of the designers stopped getting calls from Kensington Palace without any explanation from the princess. They would call up Harvey and ask her, 'Anna, what did I do wrong?' But Harvey explains that she never knew the answer: the princess made her own decisions and rarely revealed the rationale behind them.

Among the designers who found themselves working less for the princess in the late Eighties was Jacques Azagury. She did, however, begin using him again later, after he had changed his style and become far more understated, creating dresses that perfectly suited the svelte figure Diana had achieved. One day, some years after Azagury had last dressed the princess, the door of his boutique opened and Diana simply walked in. She had been driving past when she had seen some of the new designs in the window. If ever there was an example of window-dressing having the desired effect, this was it.

Azagury would go on to design some of the most successful dresses of the years after the separation, including the zip-fronted red georgette dress she wore to Venice on a 1995 trip to raise money for the Serpentine Gallery. The skirt was one of the shortest she had ever worn. Free from royal protocol, Diana increasingly gave in to designers' suggestions to push her neckline lower and her hems higher – although not as short as Azagury would have liked. He still recalls her legs as some of the most remarkable he has ever seen: 'I wanted the skirt a little shorter, but she wasn't quite ready to be that daring'.

Another less-expected casualty of Diana's reconsidered wardrobe – and one who did not come back into favour – was Bruce Oldfield. He and the princess had maintained a successful and highly productive working relationship throughout the 1980s, but by the end of the decade Diana had decided to move on. As far as Oldfield is concerned, there was no particular reason beyond the natural attenuation of a relationship between designer and customer that had matured, peaked and passed. His designs continued in the same pattern he had established – he still excels at showy occasion dresses – but the princess had decided to move in a different direction.

Oldfield believes that Diana felt she had found her own particular designer in Catherine Walker and that she decided to stick with that look. (Murray Arbeid says that in Walker, Diana 'found a glove that fitted her'.) At the time, Oldfield disagreed, and he still does. He felt that Walker's clothes were a little stiff, and that they made Diana, who was still, after all, a very young woman, look too slick and grown up, even elderly.

Although Oldfield bears no resentment toward the princess, he acknowledges that the sudden loss of her custom had a negative effect on his business. He found himself in an uncomfortable position, as, although Diana had not made his name – he was already well established when Anna Harvey had introduced him to the princess – the withdrawal of her patronage now caused damage to his reputation.

David Sassoon was another designer whose involvement with the princess eventually came to an end, in 1993. Again, there appears to have been no particular reason, although it is tempting to speculate that Sassoon's close association with the whole royal establishment may have had something to do with it. Sassoon has dressed more members of the royal family than anyone else, from Princess Alexandra to the Duchess of Kent, Princess Anne, the Queen, and Princess Alice, Duchess of Gloucester. In the intercepted telephone conversation with James Gilbey in 1991, Diana had been heard to complain about their attitude toward her: 'after all I've done for that f...ing family'. If the obscenity was an unbecoming slip of etiquette, even in a supposedly private conversation with an intimate friend, it did at least express the level of resentment Diana felt toward the royal establishment and her feeling that she had been excluded from it. Sassoon was, in his own way, an inextricable part of that establishment, so it was hardly surprising that when Diana kicked over the traces, he went too.

Catherine Walker remained the princess's most constant designer, and her small team was kept busy fulfilling the clothing needs of Diana's full public

PS 63

schedule, which did not dwindle. In one year, she had as many as 120 royal duties – only thirty fewer than the queen herself. Even without the Prince of Wales, Diana was a hugely popular royal visitor, and the adulation that greeted her was even higher on foreign visits than in Britain. Inevitably, as most of her well-wishers were women, her wardrobe was the major – if not, indeed, the only – topic of conversation.

But the idolization was beginning to wear thin for the princess. She was tired of being simply Prince Charles's wife – an increasingly fragile position in any case – and of having a reputation based entirely on her appearance. Diana had decided, in the words of her then press secretary, that she would prefer to be known as a workhorse rather than a clothes horse. He said, 'The media put the emphasis on fashion and we'd been working pretty hard to get the emphasis off fashion'.

As the first step in the process, the palace stopped issuing press releases giving details of the princess's outfits. They had for many years been an important aspect of the information provided to the press corps covering official occasions, the object being to ensure that details of what was worn were correctly listed. By deciding to drop them, the princess was giving a very clear signal that she expected to be judged on what she did rather than how she looked. She was frustrated that so many visits she made to try to raise the profile of causes in which she passionately believed boiled down to a few column inches about her clothes, and not always approving ones at that.

The gesture was highly significant, although it was soon undercut by many of Diana's designers, who had their own profiles to promote and their own PR companies for the purpose. Diana herself also undermined it: she once telephoned TV presenter Anne Diamond to make sure that the breakfast news programmes gave Catherine Walker the credit for a particularly successful dress. It was also futile, because by now it was too late. Diana had allowed her worth to be judged by her appearance, and that would never stop. Above all, it was unrealistic. Her appearance had become a national obsession.

There were a number of cases of confusion as a result of this sudden reticence about clothing. The highest profile example was when Valentino took the credit for the dress by Christina Stambolian that knocked the Prince of Wales's confession of adultery off the front pages in June 1994. Another example came in 1997, when Diana wore an ice-blue dress from Catherine

Walker and another similar piece by Jacques Azagury. When she wore the Walker to a charity auction and the Azagury the next night to the opera, photographers yelled at her for wearing the same dress two nights in a row, much to the princess's amusement.

Despite Diana's desire to change public perceptions of her and to be seen as a more serious person, her clothes remained her best method of communication. Even when she wore jeans and a jacket to visit AIDS patients, she still got more, and more positive, media attention than her husband, dressed in top hat and morning dress for Royal Ascot. In *Vogue*, Sarah Mower noted how the princess was apparently dressing increasingly for sympathy in dark clothes that made her resemble a young woman thrust into premature mourning. She observed, 'The Catherine Walker suits and coat dresses say: working woman. The evening dresses announce: royal grandeur. The dropping-Harry-at-school clothes reassure: Kensington mother'. But at the same time, *Vogue*'s sister magazine *Tatler* condemned Diana as an 'Essex girl', whose clothes and attitudes increasingly reflected the worst of English suburban taste.

CATHERINE WALKER, IN PARTICULAR, seemed to understand that Diana's clothes needed to fit with her role as a professional charity worker who was determined to use her unique position in an attempt to do good. Together, this now well-established team developed a new look for Diana: slightly softer, certainly more decorous, with far less exposed skin and often with long sleeves and higher necklines. Her skirts became straight and short and were normally worn with dark tights and jackets. She dressed explicitly to be photographed, so she had to avoid fabrics such as linen that would crumple and would show up as highly creased in photographers' flashlights. Her jackets had to be quite structured for the same reason: relaxed clothes photographed like ill-fitting sacks, unless carefully posed and lit in a photographer's studio. Designers used padding and lining to make the clothes strong enough to take the wear and tear – this was couture for working, not simply for looking at.

Diana herself began to refer to her charity duties as 'the Work', with a capital W that summed up the importance she was placing on it. The Polish-born designer Tomasz Starzewski, who began dressing the princess in 1990, ten years after he had designed the wedding dress for her sister-in-law, Victoria Lockwood, remembers, 'We found fabrics for her that looked like linen but wouldn't crumple. We would take a jacket and remount it for her, so that it wouldn't look tired by the end of the day'. Diana had been attracted to Starzewski by his trademark horizontally pleated dresses, one of which she bought from the Lucien Phillips boutique, in pink with two horizontal black bands. Diana's patronage – along with that of the Duchess of York, who bought the same dress in black – ensured Starzewski's success. He sold more than 400 dresses in the same style.

When Diana visited Japan on a goodwill tour in 1995, she wore a wardrobe of simple suits, similar to those in which Donna Karan was dressing female executives across America. She had more or less abandoned hats, though she continued to wear them on more formal occasions. She might have been any professional woman on a working visit. It was a far cry from her visit in 1986, when she had delighted the emperor and empress by adopting a Rising Sun theme to echo the national flag in a white dress with red polka dots – bought off the peg at a boutique in the Fulham Road for the precise occasion – and a broad-brimmed red straw hat by Freddie Fox.

Throughout Diana's royal career, overseas tours were one of the most high-profile, but also one of the most demanding duties, for the princess and her designers alike. As early as a 1985 tour to Australia, Diana travelled with wardrobe trunks and chests – each bearing her distinctive pink 'Princess of Wales' luggage label – containing more than twenty daytime outfits, almost as many evening dresses, dozens of pairs of shoes, and the tights, jewellery, underwear and handbags to match. Such a wardrobe usually required at least one or two dressers to maintain it: pressing, mending, sewing on buttons, and so on. The *Times* once calculated the cost of clothing for a sixteen-day trip at £80,000. Based on Diana wearing two outfits a day (in fact, she often wore more), that worked out at around £2500 per outfit.

In the early years, Jasper Conran found that the demands of creating a working wardrobe for a tour threatened to swamp everything else in his workroom. Eventually he was forced to explain to the princess that he simply could not produce the clothes she required – more than thirty outfits at the same time – and still be able to develop the collection that was the basis of his whole business. He called Diana and said to her, 'Please Ma'am, don't do this to me!' The princess understood the situation perfectly and thereafter spread her orders more thinly.

Ready-to-wear designers, such as Jasper Conran, function by creating seasonal collections. This approach is the life blood of the business, providing samples for customers and, more importantly, producing clothes that can be ordered in bulk by stockists throughout the country. Of all Diana's designers, only Catherine Walker really had the resources to devote as much time to the princess as she needed. Indeed, the bond between the pair was so strong that Walker was willing to forgo other parts of her business, even at the risk of neglecting other customers, in order to look after Diana's needs. For Walker, the exciting opportunity to dress the princess took precedence over all other business considerations. For Diana, meanwhile, it was like having a personal fashion designer who understood her precise needs without having to be told what they were, which had been the basis of all upper-class and wealthy dressing in the time of her grandmother.

In the royal tradition, Diana's designers were provided with a list of locations and events for an upcoming tour up to four months in advance. Sometimes, as with the princess's visit to the Vatican in April 1985, Catherine Walker made an advance trip herself to understand local traditions, taking an academic approach unusual among designers. At other times, she relied on reports prepared by members of the royal staff about the particular destination. Much of it was common sense, but a knowledge of local etiquette was invaluable: in particular, the demands for modesty in Muslim countries (covering head, elbows and knees and not wearing open-toed shoes) or the tradition of sitting cross-legged while eating in Bedouin tents. Sometimes, the advice was a little more straightforward. On a visit to Brazil in 1991, Diana was advised to avoid green and yellow, the colours of the Brazilian soccer team, which had lost a crucial match in the World Cup. Catherine Walker was told that the colours would be seen as 'rather gauche', and that she should also steer clear of blue and white, the colours of the Argentine team that had beaten them, as using them would 'start a riot'.

Walker's research paid dividends. For a visit to India, she decorated the top half of a dress and the accompanying bolero in beadwork reminiscent of the borders on Indian paintings or of marquetry from the time when the Islamic Mughal dynasty ruled the northern part of the country. For a trip to Dubai, she based strong shades of pink, red and gold on the traditional colours the Bedouin made from vegetable dyes. For Egypt, Walker put the princess in a tan-coloured dress reminiscent of a male safari jacket, with sleeves that covered the elbows and a hem that just covered the knees. When Diana wore a calf-length green bib-front day dress to Cairo, she produced a printed white chiffon scarf to wrap around her head à la Grace Kelly to visit the Al-Azhar mosque, covering her hair in the Islamic tradition. Walker researched batik prints from Nigeria, flowers from Indonesia, and what colours the Japanese wear for mourning. Nothing that could be anticipated was left to chance: she even held double quantities of fabric in case a sudden disaster called for a dress to be repaired or remade. And, of course, in common with all members of the royal family when travelling, Diana's wardrobe always contained mourning clothes.

On occasion, Diana wore clothes by a designer from the country she was visiting. When she went to France in November 1988, she chose to arrive in a startling red double-breasted bouclé coat by Karl Lagerfeld for Chanel, complete with forage cap and classic Chanel chain-handled handbag. On Anna Harvey's recommendation, she also selected a bright red Christian Lacroix cocktail dress in Paris. Catherine Walker, of course, was French herself – her mentor was that most Gallic of French designers, Yves Saint Laurent – and so when the princess met President and Madame Mitterand, she wore a floor-length cream coat dress with square shoulders in the Saint Laurent style.

The highlight of the Princess of Wales's 1988 Paris trip, and for some observers one of the highlights of the princess's entire official wardrobe, came from a different designer. Catherine Walker recalls wanting to see Diana in the coat dress she had designed. 'I switched on the news to watch... stupid mistake! Instead I saw the wonderful dress Victor Edelstein had made with the most beautiful embroidery'. Walker spent a sleepless night, and concedes, 'I wasn't so much jealous as energized, because it was so beautiful'. It was the Edelstein dress that convinced Walker to consider using embroidery, a departure for her but one that she would successfully incorporate into many of Diana's future outfits. Walker also notes that, typically, she got a message from Diana the next morning saying that she would be wearing Walker's clothes for the rest of the visit.

The Edelstein dress was the most expensive that the princess ever bought – it cost about £55,000 in 1998 – and it both recalled the fairytale clothing of her early royal career and demonstrated clearly how far she had

come since. It was a long formal dinner dress in oyster duchess satin, with a strapless bodice and a long-sleeved bolero. Bodice and jacket were both embroidered with sprays of carnations and birds made from simulated pearls, white paste and white bugle beads outlined in gold beads. The embroidery had been done by the Parisian firm of Hurel, time-honoured embroiderers to many of France's leading couturiers.

The effect was sensational: in its regal grandeur the dress echoed the formal gowns worn by queens and princesses, the lost worlds of Elizabeth I and Marie Antoinette, and the portraits of Winterhalter. It took the princess back into a world of formal portraits and grand palaces. It would have been at home in the Versailles of Louis XIV the Sun King, let alone the Elysée Palace. It was probably the last incarnation of Diana as the historical idea of a princess – romantic, beautiful and immaculate. And she had pulled it off in the home of haute couture, with the most critical fashion press in the world. The dress was a high-water mark of extravagance for Diana, whose wardrobe would be considerably pared down in the early 1990s, with simple sheaths and wrap dresses becoming more prominent.

For a visit to Japan in 1986, many expected the princess to observe the tradition she had established by wearing Chanel and Lacroix in France, and Escada in Germany, and wear something by a Japanese-born designer working in London. The obvious choice was Yuki, who made just the kind of unchallenging clothes in which Diana felt most comfortable. But the call from Kensington Palace never came. Embarrassed by queries from his friends and the press in Japan, Yuki mentioned the situation to a few contacts in the society world in which he chiefly operated. Eventually, word of the situation reached Diana herself, and she had her private secretary telephone to invite him to submit some sketches. Yuki went one better: he got hold of Diana's measurements from another designer and made up three dresses on spec. When Diana liked his sketches, he was able to deliver the garments there and then. Questioned on how he had managed to make them fit her so perfectly, he told her, 'I have a spy'.

In the event, Diana wore only one of the Yuki dresses in Japan – a long dress of Fortuny pleats in royal blue, with a beaded collar, which she set off by wearing a blue choker as a headband. Critics did not think that the dress flattered her, which is perhaps why she did not wear the other two.

AT THE START OF THE NINETIES, Diana began to change her hairstyle, thanks largely to Sam McKnight, with whom she first worked on a photographic session organized for *Vogue* by Anna Harvey in 1991. Diana asked the Scotsman, then one of fashion's leading hairdressers, what he would do with her hair. He suggested that by thinning it and reducing the volume, he could take five years off her appearance. The princess told him to go right ahead. The photographer was Patrick Demarchelier, who would take many of the most revealing portraits of Diana. He told *Hello!* magazine how McKnight changed the princess's hair almost instantly, making it shorter and yet more relaxed: 'She'd changed her look, found a stylist and a hair stylist... and gained a new kind of confidence'. McKnight related to Anna Harvey that he used to constantly tell Diana, 'Your hair looks fine'. He felt that she looked better with a more casual style, but the princess approached the change cautiously, saying, 'Sam, these people are expecting to see Princess Diana'.

The new shorter style was easier to maintain than the older, more formal haircut, and it suited the princess because it emphasized the length of her neck, and therefore her height. One July evening in 1991, she joined thousands of other music lovers in London's Hyde Park to enjoy an open-air concert by the tenor Luciano Pavarotti. The heavens opened and Diana, like everyone else in the audience, was soaked. Wearing a dark blue jacket by Paul Costelloe with square diamanté buttons that lent her a touch of showbiz glamour, she simply swept back her wet, tousled hair to create another iconic image of effortless style.

The new hairstyle also showed off to better advantage Diana's jewellery, particularly earrings and her trademark chokers. The princess, like most young women of her age, came to her marriage with only a few pieces of jewellery. She very quickly acquired one of the world's great collections, valued at £15 million. This is something that is only possible for the very rich who live under security protection at all times, with personal detectives and armed guards. The magnificent jewels had an important influence on Diana's wardrobe. Designers and princess together began to realize that the effects of the jewellery allowed the shape of her clothes to become much simpler: Diana's impressive body and a striking suite of jewellery would create a stunning combination. David Sassoon recalls that some of the pieces were so spectacular that the princess would ask designers to create dresses specifically to complement a particular item from her collection.

Most of the jewellery, including the Queen Mary tiara, came to Diana as gifts from members of the royal family. Prince Charles gave his wife presents of jewellery throughout their marriage. Starting with the sapphire engagement ring from Garrard, his gifts also included a heart-shaped necklace of gold and pearls and a charm bracelet made from gold, to which he regularly added charms.

The jeweller Edward Green knew the princess well: he had first worked with Diana when he was at the firm of Collingwood, the Spencer family jewellers, when her father and stepmother came in to buy a present for the young girl's sixteenth birthday. When Diana became engaged and suddenly needed jewellery for public occasions, she came to the Collingwood store on New Bond Street and selected items to borrow. Green's connection with the princess continued after he moved to Garrard, the royal jeweller. There he worked with both Prince Charles and the princess herself.

Green remembers that the prince's taste was more traditional than his wife's. The Prince of Wales had ordered for his wife a green diamond suite – necklace, earrings and bracelet – set in white gold. While the colour combination suited Diana's complexion well, Green felt that the princess herself would have preferred something a little more modern.

To achieve that more contemporary feel, Diana came up with a rather unpredictable solution. Even though she possessed some of the world's greatest jewellery, she also regularly shopped at Butler and Wilson, a London costume jeweller popular with young urban women who wanted to buy fake pearls and paste jewellery at about £20 for a pair of earrings. On any number of occasions, Diana proved just how convincing the Butler and Wilson items were. The most famous came when she appeared in the Gulf States in 1986 wearing diamanté earrings in the shape of Saudi Arabia's national symbol, the crescent moon. Most observers assumed that the earrings were a costly present from the royal couple's hosts. In fact they had been picked up for a song in London's Fulham Road.

Saudi Arabia and the Gulf were the source of some of the princess's most spectacular jewels, given to her either as wedding presents or as mementos of foreign tours to the region. Edward Green remembers, in particular, the regularly worn sapphire diamond suite that was the wedding present from Saudi Arabia. The princess also received many less traditional gifts from around the world, including a quantity of foot jewellery from countries in which such adornment is common. Although, unquestionably, it could not be worn on formal occasions, it appealed greatly to Diana's personal fashion tastes.

The princess often visited Green at Garrard, both to buy new pieces and to have old ones remade. For example, she would ask for particular stones to be taken out of brooches and set as chokers or on strings of pearls, or would request that bracelets be converted into headbands. This could be considered an exercise in frugality from a woman whose extravagance was being criticized on all sides – perhaps, at least in part, as a result of stories planted in the papers by her husband's supporters in the 'War of the Windsors'. However, given that the individual pieces were worth tens or even hundreds of thousands of pounds, perhaps frugality is not the right word.

There is a codicil to the story of Diana's jewellery: whenever the Queen is given gems as official gifts, they enter the state collection. When Diana received jewels, however, they became her own personal property. Since her death, most of the pieces have remained in storage. They will perhaps one day pass to the partners of her sons or, as Green suggests, they might even skip a generation before forming the basis of a new royal collection.

If anything happens

**do you think**

**as another**

to me,

**people will see me**

**Jackie Kennedy?**

DIANA, PRINCESS OF WALES

# diana's hair and **make-up**

Diana once mused, 'People wonder how I always look as if I've just had my hair done. It's because I have'. There, in essence, is the secret of good grooming: little and often. Diana got her hairdressers to visit her at Kensington Palace every morning, and she flew them around the world when she went on tour. More than any other member of the royal family, she appreciated the importance of looking as good as possible every time she appeared before the public. Throughout most of her life, Diana remained loyal to Kevin Shanley, her hairdresser at Head Lines, which was her regular salon before she was married. He was responsible for the much-imitated bob of her early career and for this flicked-up look.

When it came to hair styles, Diana's photograph album showed as many regrettable looks as that of any other woman of her age. Styles change, and out-of-date hair, more than anything else, can look so wrong as to be risible. Certainly, the page-boy Diana cut of the engagement period seems dated now, as does the brushed-back Forties French roll (shown right) that appeared from time to time. But in the main, Kevin Shanley and, later, Sam McKnight were able to come up with a look and stick to it with only small variations.

After Diana's divorce, Sam McKnight persuaded the princess to let him cut her hair short. The sleek, more manageable look provided an indication of the more business-like direction Diana was taking.

Barbara Daly, who did Diana's make-up for the royal wedding and went on to become one of her most frequent make-up artists, understood about putting on an appearance that would survive the glare of the lights and the relentless scrutiny of the lens. So did her client. Diana usually did her own make-up for all but formal occasions and photographic shoots and Daly found that she was a quick learner who picked up tricks easily: focus on the eyes, keep the feeling fresh rather than formal, underplay rather than overplay make-up. The make-up emphasized Diana's strengths – her tendency to blush in classic English rose fashion, her fine bone structure, her exceptional skin, her ability to be photographed to advantage from nearly any angle.

'I felt thrilled that Diana could at last control her own image. The real person had finally become strong enough to supersede the image.'

CATHERINE WALKER

# fashion **icon**

THE PRINCE AND PRINCESS OF WALES divorced on 28 August 1996, four years after their formal separation. Buckingham Palace announced that the princess would no longer be known as Princess Diana or as Your Royal Highness. In a piece of semantic nuancing as delicate as any to be found in the tsar's court in Imperial Russia, she would be known instead as Diana, Princess of Wales. It was a gesture that Diana found hurtful, and many considered spiteful, but the downgrading of her status also removed the restrictions under which she had lived for a decade and a half.

For Diana, the disengagement from her royal position had begun much earlier. Only a year after her separation from Prince Charles, on 3 December 1993, Diana chose a lunch at the Hilton Hotel in London to announce that she was withdrawing from public life. Overnight, she severed her links with many of the charities of which she was patron. Blaming the intensity of media interest for its effect on her public and private life, she signalled that her only concern now was for her two sons: 'My first priority will continue to be our children, William and Harry, who deserve as much love, care and attention as I am able to give, as well as an appreciation of the tradition into which they were born'.

Although Diana was quick to acknowledge – somewhat hypocritically in the light of later revelations of her private life – that she still had to behave like the mother of the future king (a duty that she claimed to place above all others),

Fly
Virgin
Atlantic

she no longer had to live as a member of the royal family. Nor did she have to live up to a figure that seemed increasingly remote, belonging to an already distant past. She came into her own as an individual, with strong ideas of how best to salvage her life from the debacle of the royal marriage.

Almost as significant as the announcement at the Hilton Hotel was the outfit Diana wore in which to make it. The dark green cavalry twill suit with contrasting velvet lapels was a much plainer and simpler outfit than the princess would once have worn. It was essentially the suit if not of a business executive, then certainly of a woman taking herself seriously and expecting others to do the same. It is not too fanciful to suggest that, having seen the rise of the power dresser on both sides of the Atlantic, she had realized the difference between the power that comes with position and that which comes from achievement. It was the latter that she was determined to obtain in her own right, which is why she chose to dress in a very specific way for lunch at the Hilton. But the suit was not an abrupt rupture with the past. Instead it was a symbol of a new seriousness that would show itself most clearly in her appearance.

The suit was one of Diana's first purchases from Amanda Wakeley, a new British designer who was making a name with her well-cut trouser suits and daywear. Wakeley's suit had a short, plain pencil skirt. As she says, 'Diana didn't need the bells and whistles – she had wonderful arms, great shoulders, a good bosom and good skin'. (Wakeley had reason to appreciate the effort it had taken Diana to get into such good shape: she had seen the princess working out at the gymnasium they shared at Chelsea Harbour Club.) Wakeley's clothes were unobtrusive and free of trend statements, though well made, and suited Diana's private wardrobe. Many were never seen in public. But they had texture – from suede, cashmeres and silks – and a flattering cut that made the wearer feel relaxed and confident. Diana was increasingly coming to believe that glamour came from within, not from her clothing. As Roland Klein says, 'She was the statement, not the clothes. If the frock becomes the statement, you've failed as a designer'.

As she took what she called 'time and space' over the next year or so, Diana focused on the charities that particularly concerned her. She also became more accustomed to living independently. Increasingly, she was comfortable being photographed in everyday wear: jeans and sunglasses while on a shopping trip, a sweatshirt and shorts for the health club, and a large, enveloping soft coat and cashmere scarf for a trip to her therapist or astrologer. In clothes terms, the wheel had come full circle: Diana had reverted to her class, dressing in the uniform of the hip modern Sloane Ranger.

But, in a possibly subconscious parallel movement, Diana was edging towards a new international fashion code which said not only that casual was cool, but also that cheap labels with the right street credentials can say much more than grand ones. Wealthy women around the world mixed the two – a Polo Ralph Lauren shirt with a Stussy baseball cap, for example. Increasingly dazzled by the glamour of American upper-class life, she was especially beguiled by how wealthy New Yorkers lived. To find their secret, she avidly flicked through U.S. society magazines such as *Town & Country* and *Vanity Fair*.

Always she was desperately trying to find her own path. At home inside Kensington Palace, according to Paul Burrell, Diana was often lonely and withdrawn. On a trip to Chicago in 1996, Diana replied to a journalist who had admired her ability to shake hands constantly and meet thousands of new people, 'This is the easy part. The hard part is tomorrow night when I'm home in an empty house'. In public, however, she remained highly positive and remarkably popular.

WHEN DIANA WORE CHRISTINA STAMBOLIAN'S sexy little black dress to upstage Prince Charles's TV confession of adultery in June 1994 – as part of a concerted campaign by the prince's advisers to claw back some of the ground he had lost to his estranged wife – newspapers everywhere put her on the front page. The moment marked Diana's return to the limelight after her self-imposed exile. Stambolian remembers the dress with affection. The princess had bought it two years before the event, calling in at Stambolian's boutique after lunch with her brother, Charles, and announcing that she needed a dress for a special occasion. What that occasion might be, Diana did not say, and it may well be that she had no real idea at the time. At the urging of the designer and of Earl Spencer, Diana settled on a shorter dress than she was used to, and chose it in black – she dismissed the other choice, white, as being too virginal.

The dress then hung in Diana's walk-in dressing room at Kensington Palace until the night of the Prince Charles broadcast, when Valentino angered her and Anna Harvey with his unchecked advance press release.

As he had broken protocol by releasing details of her outfit in advance, Diana at once decided to abandon the Valentino, and replaced it with the unworn Stambolian dress. She completed the look with a pearl choker with a large oval sapphire – a favourite piece she had been given by the Queen Mother – and walked back into public life. The next morning, the front page of the *Daily Mirror* featured a photograph of Diana below the headline 'Take That!'

There is a postscript to the tale of the Christina Stambolian dress: the designer received no credit for it. Because Valentino had released details of the dress without waiting to check whether it would be worn, and did not withdraw the erroneous press release, the newspapers almost universally credited Diana's outfit to the Italian couturier. Stambolian's business was struggling, and she could have benefited from such spectacular publicity – as many other British designers had profited from being associated with Diana – but it was not to be. It was an incident that can be taken as a salutary reminder of the high stakes involved in dressing the Princess of Wales. It is also worth noting that, just as Diana never bought anything else from Stambolian, so she only ever wore one dress by Valentino.

Stambolian, like Amanda Wakeley, was a new designer for Diana, and reflected the princess's fresher, simpler style. Theirs were clothes for executives, young mothers, women who felt good about themselves. Shapes were basic, and relied on a softer cut rather than on strong outlines or adornment. Diana's new clothes allowed her to make more of her body. Roland Klein remembers that one of the last dresses she ordered from him – a loose style reminiscent of 1920s' evening wear – originally reached the mid calf. Diana asked him to shorten it, and then to shorten it again, until eventually the designer said to her, 'Don't you think it's a little too short?'. The princess replied, 'Look, whatever I do I'll be criticized, so let's go for it'. It was a far cry from the days when she had resisted the urgings of Bruce Oldfield to show more of her legs. (Oldfield says that he once tried to persuade her by showing her a photograph of Princess Margaret in the Sixties wearing what was virtually a mini skirt. Diana laughed and remarked, 'Perhaps Margaret didn't have the paparazzi kneeling on the pavement ready to photograph her every time the car door was opened'.)

Diana's new style also relied more than previously on foreign designers. It is an old canard that she was not allowed to wear anything other than British clothes while she was a member of the royal family. As early as 1991, she was photographed joyously greeting her sons on board the royal yacht *Britannia* after a foreign trip wearing a red, white and black Moschino suit, which she also selected for the christening of Princess Eugenie the following year. She had worn clothes from French, Italian and other designers for some time, and had always made a feature of dressing in the clothes of appropriate designers for overseas trips. It meant as much to these foreign designers as it did to their British counterparts. In 1995, Christian Lacroix wrote to Anna Harvey to thank her for her assistance in arranging the princess's presence at a function.

Meanwhile, some of the so-called British fashion in which the princess dressed was British only in that its designers happened to be working in London. Despite the urgings of the British Fashion Council and others to the contrary, the clothes of Roland Klein and Catherine Walker were largely French in spirit, while Jean Vanvelden was of Dutch extraction, Stambolian Greek, Azagury Moroccan, Starzewski Polish and Yuki just as much Japanese as he was English. Diana's clothes always reflected a wide range of influences, including the varied ethnic backgrounds of her designers, not to mention her desire to compliment the cultures of the countries she visited.

Diana continued to be served well by some of her established couturiers, notably Jacques Azagury, Catherine Walker, Victor Edelstein and Roland Klein. Azagury, for example, provided a low-cut black gown that she wore to a London dinner held on the same night in November 1995 that her own dramatic TV contribution to the 'War of the Windsors' was broadcast. Diana had secretly contacted and given an interview to the BBC *Panorama* journalist Martin Bashir. It contained more revelations about the misery behind the royal marriage, and a sensational admission from the princess that she had indeed been unfaithful to her husband with the cavalry officer James Hewitt. In another example of her ability to shape her appearance, Diana wore simple, barely noticeable clothes, and used her make-up to give her a somewhat doleful air, with large puppy eyes. It was the height of what *Tatler* had dubbed her 'sympathy dressing'.

Meanwhile, however, while millions were glued to the broadcast – with bitterly ironic timing it fell on the Queen's wedding anniversary – Diana was appearing before the cameras in Azagury's black dress with a lavishly embroidered bodice scattered with sequins. She was clearly aware of the

sensational effect of the dress: when the designer had first shown it to her, she had commented, 'That's a bit of a sexy dress, Jacques'. Azagury could only agree. Diana found out for herself the perils of this new, sexier style of dressing when she wore the same gown a few weeks later to receive an award from former secretary of state Henry Kissinger in New York for her humanitarian work. It is said that Kissinger's admiration of Diana's cleavage – which could not have been much below the level of his nose – was perhaps a little too obvious.

SOME OF DIANA'S MOST SUCCESSFUL NEW CLOTHES came from abroad. For example, Chanel and Lacroix in Paris were making well-cut, flattering but modest clothes suitable for the high-profile international figure Diana had become. Most notably and successfully of all, she formed an unlikely collaboration with Versace. Trained originally by his dressmaker mother, Gianni Versace had established himself as probably the most creative designer in Italy. But he was also couture's bad boy par excellence, with a reputation for louche excess – a combination of buccaneer, highwayman and the Marquis de Sade. In his constant search for a balance between elegance and sexiness, he had tipped many times into vulgarity, with bold and startling uses of colour that varied from sensational to tarty. His style also made deliberately provocative use of materials such as soft metals and leather, with their well-known fetishistic overtones. Versace based all of his shapes on the perfect female body, and his insistence on and interest in physical perfection bordered on totalitarian.

It would have caused all sorts of embarrassment for Diana to be publicly associated with Versace while she was a royal princess. Now that she was independent, however, she suffered no such qualms. She was introduced to the designer by her hair stylist, Sam McKnight, who worked on Versace's shows. Anna Harvey recalls that McKnight was so eager to get princess and couturier together that he showed Diana a photograph of Christy Turlington in a pale blue Versace dress with heavy beading. Diana ordered the dress and liked it so much that when she was preparing for a trip to New York, she went back to Versace. From a photograph, she ordered a white jersey dress covered in rhinestones – the model this time was Naomi Campbell – which looked sensational. Fashion does not always work at long distance, however. Just before the trip, the dress arrived to great excitement, but Versace had sent the wrong garment. What arrived was so completely wrong for the princess that she and Anna Harvey could not help laughing. Diana returned the dress with a charming note excusing everyone from any error.

The more sensational, flamboyant side of Versace's clothes was never something with which Diana would have been associated. Their relationship was more that of a master couturier with one of his ideal muses – Diana was now a dress size 12, and a highly feminine 36–26–37½. Versace had always been more Elle MacPherson and Cindy Crawford than Kate Moss. He was one of the few designers in the Eighties and Nineties who insisted on the importance of the breasts at a time when other designers sought to downplay or ignore them as either a distraction from silhouette or an unwelcome weakening of the power-dressing effect. Versace himself acknowledged Diana's combination of emotional sympathy and sensuality when he called her 'the Mother Teresa and Cindy Crawford of our time'.

Versace was a master cutter, often working on the bias and draping fabric straight onto a model, without any sketches or designs. For Diana, he produced many simple shift dresses and pastel-toned suits with fitted jackets and short pencil skirts. They gave length to her body by holding in her torso and used careful boning and underpinning to push up her breasts – the newspapers commented regularly on Diana's newly prominent cleavage – which he further emphasized with low décolletage. The dresses owed more to the tailoring of Coco Chanel – a couturier for whom Versace had no great admiration as a creative mind, but whose technical ability he could hardly fail to rate – than they did to Versace's own catwalk excesses, although Diana chose several understated elegant garments from his couture range.

Versace's smart daywear became Diana's signature wardrobe during the last few years of her life. In London, Catherine Walker and Jacques Azagury were coming up with similarly tailored but straightforward day clothes, which fitted well into the 'less is more' spirit that many designers had adopted by the middle of the Nineties. Diana wore, for example, a long brown wool double-breasted pinstripe jacket by Catherine Walker when she met Hillary Clinton for breakfast at the White House in September 1996, and looked every inch the professional when she was photographed wearing a Ralph Lauren pinstripe dark suit striding alongside the designer.

THE NEW, SHORTER AND SIMPLER SKIRTS made more of a show of Diana's legs – they were kept permanently bronzed by judicious use of a sun bed – and the effect was complemented by a change in footwear. Always slightly embarrassed about her height, particularly when she was standing next to her husband who was barely taller than her, Diana had frequently worn flat pumps throughout her marriage. As she became more of her own woman, and more confident about her body, she began to wear higher heels. To make the most of her ankles, she commissioned footwear from the world's leading shoemakers. Both were based in London but, like many of Diana's other favourite designers, both were of foreign extraction. Manolo Blahnik, who had made shoes for Diana throughout her marriage, was Spanish by birth – he grew up in the Canary Islands – while Jimmy Choo was a shy, gentle, Malaysian-born cobbler working in the East End.

Blahnik made shoes in the tradition of his hero Roger Vivier, combining remarkable creativity with a fine understanding of balance and anatomy to create shoes that were daring, sexy and yet comfortable to wear. At least one pair of 'Manolos' was de rigueur for the wardrobe of any international super-rich woman. (Diana's divorce settlement of a rumoured £17 million guaranteed her financial independence for life.) The enthusiasm of his American clientele reached such heights that some devotees were known to buy two pairs of a favourite style, one to wear and one to have on display to be admired. True aficionados could get both pairs signed by the designer on his annual promotional tours across the States, which triggered a feeding-frenzy from New York to California.

Choo's trademark was a soft pump with a small V cut into the front, but he, too, was able to combine stability with high-heeled, strappy shapes to make spectacular formal shoes that were easy to walk in. Even so, he often warned Diana when a pair of shoes might cause particular problems for her, although her early dance training had given her such a sure sense of balance that he need not have worried. Choo made most of his shoes for the princess after her separation from Prince Charles. Styles ranged from trademark flat pumps to flat leather day shoes and more glamorous high heels: 'Her favourites were high-heel strappy shoes. She liked classic styles', recalls Choo. Every few months, Diana would call him to come to Kensington Palace, where they would discuss styles and she would show him examples of the fabrics she would be wearing.

Afterwards, she would help him pack the bagfuls of samples back into the car, much to his embarrassment – 'I have an old banger'.

Hats changed along with shoes. At heart, Diana had never particularly liked wearing hats, but she had never felt that she could dispense with them altogether in the way she had gloves. She had a well-developed sense of what people expected when they met her, and she knew that the public would be disappointed if she arrived at an official occasion without a hat. After her separation, however, the princess wore hats only rarely, and when she did, she abandoned the large-brimmed creations that had once been typical. Instead, she asked Philip Somerville to make her a collection of pillbox hats to sit high on the back of her head so that they showed her fringe and her entire face.

As Diana gave her occasional speeches about the charities and issues with which she was still closely involved – Barnardos, HIV/AIDS and, increasingly, land mines – the pastel Versace and Walker suits, often in textured wool, and the pillbox hats inevitably recalled Jackie Kennedy. Both as a style icon and as a symbol of an independent woman who had overcome tragedy to achieve contentment and a place in a nation's hearts, Jackie Kennedy was one of Diana's heroines. Versace even designed what must have been a deliberate pastiche of a Jackie Kennedy suit in pink, which Diana wore on a visit to Argentina.

OTHER HEROINES CAME FROM HOLLYWOOD. The press observed disapprovingly at times that Diana seemed to present herself and behave in a style more reminiscent of a starlet than of a former member of the royal family. *The Sunday Telegraph* called her 'trivial and self-indulgent' and 'a café society jetsetter'. There was a report that the princess had become fascinated by supermodels, the glamour stars of the 1990s, and had even asked to meet Linda Evangelista to talk about modelling.

She started using fashion photographers rather than society photographers for her official portraits. Jacques Azagury remembers her showing him the first pictures taken of her by Mario Testino, the Peruvian who is on every designer's A list of photographers. Testino captured Diana's new sexuality and confidence. She told Azagury, 'Mario has shown me how to catwalk', and gave him a small demonstration, strutting around the room. As one of the great flatterers, Testino quickly became one of Diana's favourite photographers, along with

Terence Donovan and Patrick Demarchelier. With them, she enjoyed a relaxed, intimate relationship, sitting around in their studios and gossiping.

Diana's comfort in front of the camera was hard won. At the very start of her career, her favoured photographer was Lord Snowdon, who, as the former husband of Princess Margaret, had some understanding of and sympathy for the demands of marriage into the royal family. Snowdon had taken the first portraits of Diana for British *Vogue*, even before the engagement, and followed them with a series of official portraits of the princess, for the engagement, her twenty-first birthday, and the births of both her sons. Snowdon specialized in somewhat formal portraits for the princess; it was a genre he understood implicitly, having spent decades in royal circles. The relationship lasted throughout her career. In 1997, when Diana decided to sell off many of her old dresses for charity, it was Snowdon she asked to take formal photographs of her wearing a half dozen of the gowns for the official catalogue.

With his insider's view, Snowdon, who also took many informal shots of Diana, was, not surprisingly, one of the most perceptive chroniclers of Diana's discomfort within the royal family. In 1991, for example, he posed Diana, Charles and their sons, Princes William and Harry, out of doors enjoying a picnic in the shade of a tree in an arrangement that owed more to Sir Joshua Reynolds than to the late twentieth century. In her riding boots, corduroys and tweed jacket, Diana looks stiff and apprehensive – as well she might. Snowdon brought a horse (held by Prince Harry) into the picture. Its presence only unsettled her more and increased the tension evident in the strained poses of husband and wife. The young urban Diana could not be more out of place in this hunting–shooting–fishing scene. To anyone sensitive to its subtle clues, Snowdon's photograph is a masterly study in estrangement and the artificiality of the royal marriage.

Other photographers worked with the princess in different ways. It was while she was preparing the catalogue for the Christies auction that Diana first used Testino, at the suggestion of her collaborator on the sale, former journalist Meredith Etherington-Smith. It was to be a brief association, but Testino proved to be uniquely capable of capturing Diana's new quicksilver sense of freedom. In the photographs published in *Vanity Fair* shortly before the auction, Testino portrayed a young superstar who was athletic, and full of humour and energy. Testino's Diana could have stepped from the pages of virtually any fashion or

celebrity magazine; the photographs have the flavour of stills taken from pop videos in which everyone is having a good time. Etherington-Smith remembers a day of laughter during the shoot at an old school in Battersea, London. Diana happily clowned around, perfecting her new runway walk, and confided to her colleague, 'That was one of the happiest days of my entire life'. When she showed Paul Burrell the photographs, she asked him, 'Don't you think I look a little like Marilyn Monroe?'

Another photographer who managed to locate Diana's sense of humour was Terence Donovan. Even in his formal portraits – a number appear in the Christies catalogue – the princess has a smile playing around the corner of her lips, as if she has just been told a rather risqué joke, which in all probability was the case. Donovan made Diana laugh very easily, and perhaps for that reason did more official portraits than anyone else. The Princess had needed dozens and dozens throughout her royal career, because they were always exchanged with visiting dignitaries as gifts. Diana became very close to the London photographer and his wife, and attended his funeral early in 1997.

Patrick Demarchelier, being French, had no false deference; he was always flirtatious with the princess, which she greatly enjoyed. Demarchelier took his first photographs of Diana in 1989 and quickly became very close to his subject. When the princess wanted to go on holiday without the press following, he loaned her his house on the exclusive Caribbean island of Saint-Barthélemy. Demarchelier's images skilfully bridged the gap between regal and relaxed. In 1990, he photographed Diana laughing in a gown with her shoulders bare and only a tiara to indicate her royal status. The portrait suggested a sensuality – highlighted by the exposed skin – that had not been seen in the princess before. *Vogue*, which had commissioned the shoot, wanted to use the image as a cover, but the Queen, who clearly saw the danger in the new informality, vetoed the idea.

The photographer who probably took more images of Diana than anyone else was Tim Graham. He began by following her around the world as just another member of the press corps but has become acknowledged as the source of the most comprehensive collection of images of Diana's clothes. It is a testament to the close relationship between Graham and the princess – indeed, between the princess and photographers in general – that far from being despised as a member of the paparazzi, Graham was accepted and even invited to take informal portraits

of Diana and her family. In the early 1980s, he was granted exclusive access to the family to take photographs for a book to raise funds for the Princes Trust charities, *In Private, In Public: The Prince and Princess of Wales*.

In autumn 1994, Catherine Walker echoed Diana's interest in the elegance of the past in a collection that experimented with what she called 'drop-dead Hollywood glamour'. Diana chose a halter-neck dress in black Clerici silk crêpe, edged in black bugle bead marquetry to frame the face and the neck. Walker noted in her autobiography, 'It was our first "sexy" dress'. Diana caused a sensation when she wore it to a gala at the Palace of Versailles organized by UNESCO in support of children's charities. Designer Pierre Cardin observed appreciatively, 'This is the home of the Sun King of France, now we have the Sun Princess of Versailles'.

When the dress was selected by *Hello!* magazine readers as Diana's most successful outfit from the previous year, the magazine remarked that the dress cast Diana as a wronged wife in part because it was cut 'in the style favoured by the most stylish example of that ilk, Jackie O'. Meanwhile, at home in Kensington Palace, in another echo of a bygone age of Hollywood glamour, Diana kept framed photographs of herself dressed as a Fifties' Audrey Hepburn in costumes designed for the movie *Breakfast at Tiffany's*. On more than one occasion, Diana recognized echoes of the clothes of Hubert de Givenchy in garments that her own designers showed her, remarking, 'Very Audrey Hepburn'.

Jackie Kennedy and Audrey Hepburn: both women were obvious heroines for Diana. The great style icons of their age, and the most influential fashion leaders in America, they had nevertheless achieved widespread popularity for their good works, kindness, humour and understanding, for the personality that they projected through the media to millions of people who would never meet them. Both operated under the same constraints as Diana – even free of the royal family, it was necessary for her to avoid scandal.

Audrey Hepburn's appeal for the princess was obvious. Not only had the actress come to define chic, but also, from 1988 until her death in 1993, she acted as a goodwill ambassador for UNICEF, the United Nations' children's charity. Although she was the highest profile representative of UNICEF, Hepburn was more than a figurehead. She made more than fifty field trips to study the conditions in which children lived, and reported back to the United Nations from countries in Africa, Asia and Central America that she visited –

sometimes at a certain personal risk. At the same time, however, she did not compromise her own style, always appearing smart and yet approachable in a uniform of slacks and plain white shirts.

Audrey Hepburn was so successful in this role that she inevitably served as a model for Diana once the princess decided to begin her own practical fieldwork. Diana followed in her footsteps, even visiting some of the same countries, such as Ethiopia, wearing practical ensembles of plain white shirt, khakis and moccasins. One could quite legitimately claim that, by the end of her life, Diana was on her way to becoming a second Audrey Hepburn: a private individual who, through beauty, charm, unfailing dedication to duty and sheer determination, was able to make a difference on a national if not a global scale.

Jackie Kennedy was another role model for the princess. Paul Burrell recalled in 2006 that Diana had been for years a huge fan of Jackie, possibly at least in part because she recognized the parallel in the way in which their public careers had been cut short, one by violence and the other by divorce. Burrell said that Diana was an admirer of Nancy Reagan and Hillary Clinton, 'but Jackie Onassis had the edge'. Diana also pinpointed Jackie's son, John F. Kennedy, Jr, as an example for her own son to follow, telling *New Yorker* magazine that she hoped that Prince William would demonstrate a similar skill in handling the media.

According to Burrell, part of Diana's fascination went beyond the simple acknowledgement of Jackie's powerful sense of style and the parallels in their careers. Late in her life, Diana began to muse about the possibility of becoming First Lady herself, perhaps by pairing up with a rich American partner with political ambitions. The idea of such huge potential influence was highly attractive for a woman so committed to the idea of changing the world. There was a more practical side, too. Burrell remarked, 'She fantasized about redecorating the White House'.

In her turn, Jackie Kennedy was reported to watch Diana's career with admiration – and no doubt with some sympathy as she followed the young woman's efforts to carve out her own public role. Jackie's biographer Christopher Anderson noted that she found the princess 'beautiful, elegant, charming, very stylish'. More rewarding to Diana would have been Jackie's acknowledgement that she was a 'wonderful mother'. Still, the mutual admiration between the two

women did not affect Diana's response to an approach from Jackie, then an editor at the New York publishing firm of Doubleday, to get Diana to write an autobiography. The suggestion was turned down.

Diana was less successful than her role model in avoiding scandal, however. Stories swirled around the media of her various romantic relationships, which included a highly publicized liaison with the England rugby captain, Will Carling, and of bizarre behaviour in which Diana persistently telephoned a married man, hanging up the phone whenever his wife answered. Paul Burrell noted the arrival and departure of various suitors; although he hints that one was more important to the princess than the others, he refuses to name any names.

Outside her personal life, Diana still adhered to behaviour she perceived as appropriate for the mother of the future king. It was this adherence that led to a sudden rift with her new favourite, Gianni Versace. Versace had the talent to make quiet, comfortable clothes, but he also had an irresistible impulse to scream from the rooftops and drop his leather trousers to display his behind to the world. His publicity had often been outrageous – although admittedly fairly harmless – and when he conceived the idea of *Rock and Royalty*, it was as an iconoclastic comment on the status of true celebrity in the Nineties. The book combined images of supermodels and men wearing crowns and little else with pictures of Diana's former in-laws. In the worlds of fashion or of art, the book was unlikely to be considered much more than a somewhat provocative mishmash.

For Diana, however, Versace's book was beyond the pale. Already under attack in the media, she could not associate herself with it, even though she had previously promised to contribute a foreword on the grounds that the book would raise money for Elton John's AIDS charity. Shortly before the gala that Versace planned to launch the book, Diana withdrew her support and refused to attend as guest of honour. The dinner was cancelled, although Versace went ahead with the book. The rift between princess and designer had still not been reconciled six months later, in July 1997, when Gianni Versace was murdered on the steps of his home in Miami. His killer, a rent boy wanted in connection with a series of murders of affluent gay men, was later surrounded by police and shot himself with the same gun that killed Versace, taking to the grave any explanation of why he had targeted the designer. Diana, who made a tearful appearance at the funeral with their mutual friend Elton John, professed herself devastated by the loss of what she called 'a great and talented man'. One of the most gifted and imaginative couturiers of his generation – and the man who had played a crucial role in lifting Italian fashion from the doldrums – was dead at the age of only fifty.

IT IS A NOTABLE OMISSION from Diana's wardrobe that she rarely wore in public clothes by American designers. There was no shortage of choice, particularly in the high-end daywear provided by Donna Karan and Ralph Lauren. In fact, Diana was the perfection of the Ralph Lauren dream of class. He admired her greatly, and ever since her marriage, she had returned the compliment by wearing his clothes off duty. She also wore casual wear by Donna Karan, for whose relaxed Amazonian exercises in chic understated confidence her figure was perfect.

It might be conceded that the Europeans perhaps understood better the requirements of evening wear for a princess, which, while elegant and glamorous, should never be brash or vulgar. Indeed, it seems that glamour was something that designers generally had lost the gift of creating. As Diana Vreeland, legendary editor of American *Vogue* and the doyenne of fashion commentators, lamented as early as the Sixties, 'There are no glamorous dresses now, because there are no glamorous places. There are no rooms to fill'.

Toward the end of her life, however, Diana's more international lifestyle inevitably brought her more exposure in the United States. Her career had taken on a showbusiness quality: the removal of her royal status had placed on her an unaccustomed pressure to market herself, like any other celebrity. It was almost as if, like British bands, actors or writers, she had to 'break' America in order to be taken seriously. Admittedly, Diana was usually using her own profile in order to gain support for causes that she championed, but she had always paid attention to her own portrayal in the media and it was personally gratifying for her to keep herself in the public eye. Diana was undeniably part of a commercial package that the public would either 'buy' or not.

It was no coincidence that two of Diana's most memorable fashion moments late in her life occurred in New York. The city is the centre of U.S. fashion – although it remains a poor cousin to Paris and Milan in terms of original creativity – but also of the international jetset to which Diana increasingly belonged, and like whom she increasingly dressed. It is also the

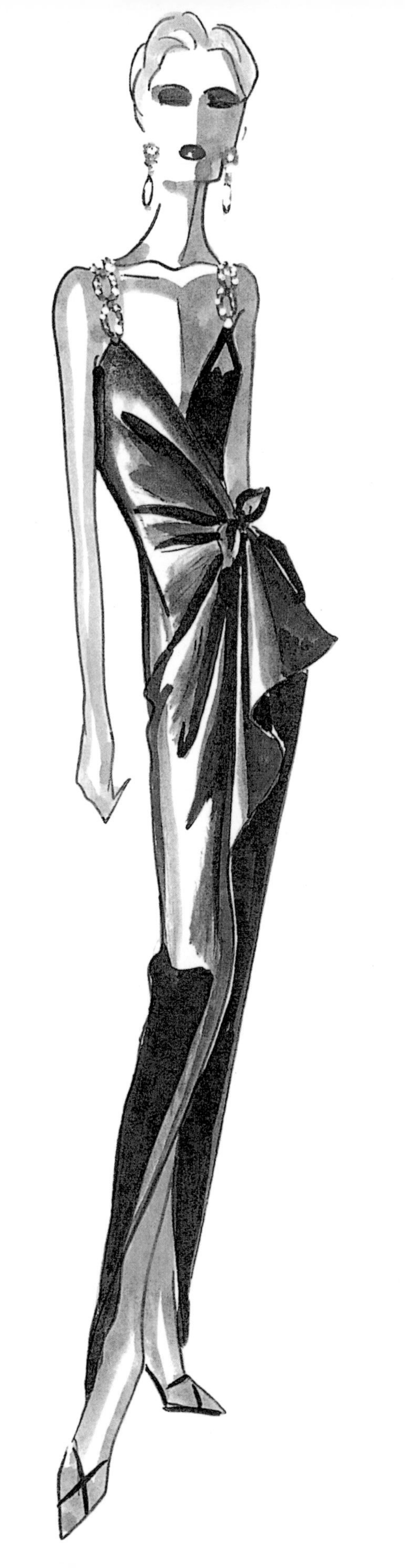

Bellville Sassoon
1993.

centre of wealth used to support charitable causes, and a compulsory stop for all committed fundraisers who want to rub shoulders with potential donors.

The Americans already loved Diana, partly because of their sneaking republican fascination with royalty, partly because of their open awe for centuries-old tradition and pomp, and partly because the story of the princess's private life was as compulsively unlikely as the sad and emotional tales spilled out to Oprah or any of her daytime TV counterparts. The removal of the title Her Royal Highness was a heraldic detail that did little to undermine Diana's status in the United States, where she was still treated with as much ceremony as ever.

In February 1995, Diana was invited to a gala for the Council for Fashion Designers of America at the Lincoln Center in New York. It was her first major fashion event outside London, but the invitation came from a special source. Liz Tilberis, former editor of British *Vogue*, had moved to New York in 1992 to become editor of *Harper's Bazaar*. Diana had first met her in 1991, when Tilberis had brought the princess together with photographer Patrick Demarchelier and hairdresser Sam McKnight for the first in a series of highly successful photographic sessions with Diana for *Vogue*. Tilberis and Diana had become firm friends – Diana felt very comfortable in the company of female journalists such as Tilberis, Anna Wintour, Anna Harvey and Tina Brown – and their friendship had become closer after Tilberis was diagnosed with ovarian cancer. Tilberis won Diana's admiration for the way she coped with her disease. (After major surgery, even though she was in an isolation ward, she had staff from *Harper's* take her magazine layouts to the hospital so that they could hold them up for her to study and comment on.) The friendship continued until Diana's death. In her autobiography, *No Time to Die*, Tilberis remembers receiving a fax from Diana agreeing to write the foreword for the book, only to learn a few days later of the princess's tragic death.

Diana agreed to attend the CFDA gala specifically to present Tilberis with an award. To appear for the first time in front of all of the United States' most fashionable people and leading designers, and to make her first speech in America, she fell back on the trusted Catherine Walker for a halter-neck navy crêpe dress with eyecatching crisscross cording across the back in silk satin duchess. Tilberis, who died in 1999, wrote in her autobiography: 'That night she looked stunning, wearing a long, royal-blue body-hugging sheath with straps crossed at the back, like a bathing suit, from her favourite designer Catherine Walker'. Diana had also changed her hairstyle for the occasion, adopting a slicked-back wet look that seemed to be trying to recapture the easy glamour of the night she had been soaked at Pavarotti's open-air concert in Hyde Park. The hairstyle was not universally judged a success – in the words of one commentator, it made Diana look as if she had just stepped out of the shower. Still, Tilberis recorded the princess's triumph: 'The "been there, done that" New York fashion crowd stopped dead in their tracks'.

With one appearance, Diana had stepped firmly into the international world of which New York was the heart. The fashionable elite of America welcomed her as one of their own – someone they could shelter from the vicissitudes and unfairness of her life at home. 'Move to New York', yelled one excited convert to Diana as she prepared to hand Tilberis her award. It was at that moment, if not before, that Diana stopped being a representative of Britain and took over a more exclusive role – and possibly a more demanding one – of being the ambassador for the fashionable across the globe, the figurehead of taste, style and more than a little sexiness.

In December 1996, Diana was back in New York with Liz Tilberis. This time she was guest of honour at a benefit dinner at the Metropolitan Museum of Art to raise money for its Costume Institute. New York's most fashionable played their part, each paying up to a thousand dollars for the privilege of a seat at what quickly became one of the social events of the year. Such an occasion cried out for something very special: Diana would have to be – was obliged to be – the belle of the ball.

Anna Harvey recalls that the story of the choice of dress for that evening began when Diana met Bernard Arnault, the president of LVMH, the company that owns Dior, Chanel, Louis Vuitton and other prestigious French brands such as Moët et Chandon and Hennessy. Arnault has allied his company to what he called the '*art de vivre*' around the world, and sees its mission as a combination of elegance and creativity. The princess had never worn much Dior – when she wore French designers, she tended to wear Chanel or Lacroix – but Arnault is nothing if not persuasive. Dior had recently released the Italian Gianfranco Ferré as its chief designer and had hired the mercurial young English designer John Galliano. The occasion gave Diana the ideal opportunity to support the most talented couturier to emerge from London fashion for at

least thirty years. After consulting with Anna Harvey, who confirmed Galliano's meteoric talent, Diana agreed to wear a Galliano couture dress for Dior.

The result was something unexpected that represented a misstep by both the princess and the designer. Although Diana looked best in carefully structured clothes, Galliano dressed her in a navy slip dress that had virtually no shaping. It made her chest look flat and her hips a little broad.

The press pounced. The criticism – which included the comment that Diana looked as if she had dropped in on the function while she was getting ready for bed, with her nightdress already on – was cruel. Galliano, forgetting that even the greatest couturier remains a tradesman for his clients, judged that the fault was with the customer, not with him: Diana had worn the dress wrongly, he claimed. As for the princess, she bore the criticism with good humour, but she did not return to Dior.

Whether she would eventually have made her peace with the label is impossible to say, of course. But for now, she responded by turning back to a designer she felt could be trusted to understand her needs. Jacques Azagury began to create for her a series of sensational evening dresses. By this time, he was a much improved designer. Since his earliest collaborations with the princess, he had developed both the judgement and the technical skill to enable him to trust in his ability to use simple, soft shapes to clothe the body. In 1997, he designed an eyecatchingly short, ice-blue sequin-covered dress for the princess to wear to a performance of *Swan Lake* by the English Ballet at the Royal Albert Hall in London, while for a New York charity gala in aid of the Red Cross, he put her in a red sash-trimmed dress in honour of the organization. The dress had a high neckline; Azagury remembers, 'She wanted people to concentrate on what she had to say, so the dress had to be serious but to have a sexy twist'. That twist was at the back: a deep V shape that would turn heads while the princess was dancing.

Diana was putting together a new wardrobe for a new role. As Jasper Conran notes, she had become very European and had also managed to divorce herself from the traditions of her class. She made room for it by throwing out the old. For the most famous clothes horse in the world, the Oxfam shop or the car-boot sale were not options – although throughout her career, Diana had given away bagfuls of old clothes to her sisters, her friends, Paul Burrell's wife and her staff. Instead, at the suggestion of her son William, Diana decided to auction seventy-nine of her past evening gowns to raise money for the Royal Marsden Hospital Cancer Fund and the AIDS Crisis Trust. She would turn couture – one of the forms of expenditure most derided as wasteful and useless – into hard cash that could do some practical good. As Christie's expert Meredith Etherington-Smith expressed it in the slogan she coined to promote the sale, 'Sequins save lives'.

In her book *Diana – The Last Word*, Simone Simmons, an energy healer and one of Diana's most controversial spiritual advisers, described joining the princess to sort out which dresses were to be sold. Many, she reports, were rediscovered with much head-shaking and cries of, 'How on earth could I have worn something like this?' The princess admitted that she had probably tried too hard to wear clothes she thought the royal family would approve of, telling Simmons, 'The Queen Mother had terrible taste, which is why I looked so awful'.

This was the comment of a woman talking about chapters of her life that have passed – Diana classed the gowns into her 'fairy period' or her 'Hollywood period'. When the dresses were selected, however, she felt a pang of loss at the prospect of parting with them, until Simmons reminded her of the importance of taking this step for moving into a new phase of her life. Many of the signature dresses from Diana's career were up for auction: the black Christina Stambolian she had worn on the night of Prince Charles's documentary; the black Victor Edelstein, in which she had danced with John Travolta at the White House; the famous Catherine Walker 'Elvis dress', with its high sequined collar; the Walker dress that had caused such a sensation at the CFDA awards in New York. There were other dresses, by Bruce Oldfield, Bellville Sassoon, Jacques Azagury, Murray Arbeid and Zandra Rhodes.

There could be little doubt about Diana's message: out with the old, in with the new. She wrote in a press release for the sale: 'Words cannot adequately describe my absolute delight at the benefits which the results of this auction will bring to so many people who need support'. The designers, the majority of whom had fallen from grace to some extent with the princess, were for the most part equally delighted. Of Diana's old favourites, only Catherine Walker dressed her throughout her career; Anna Harvey observed that even the ultra-loyal Walker was a little put out when the princess began ordering so many of her clothes from Versace in the last years of her life. Any resentment did not show, however. Walker, who herself had been diagnosed

JOHNSON

with breast cancer in 1995, proclaimed 'I am deeply moved that my designs, through the Princess, are now being used to save lives'.

Diana and Meredith Etherington-Smith, with whom she collaborated, jotted down notes for the catalogue about each of the dresses. Diana also agreed to be photographed in some of her favourite gowns and to attend previews to promote the sale both in London and New York. She added a handwritten note to use as the frontispiece of the catalogue: 'The inspiration for this wonderful sale comes from just one person ... our son William'.

When the time came in June, the clothes Diana chose to wear to promote the sale spoke volumes: in London she wore a pale blue embroidered shift dress with a plunge front by Catherine Walker; in New York, she wore another Catherine Walker dress of an almost identical cut beaded with pale floral patterns. The choice was appropriate, because Walker was by far the best-represented designer in the sale, with about fifty outfits. Both the new dresses accentuated her legs, shoulders, arms and bust – this was perhaps the real Diana saying goodbye to all of the former Dianas she had once been.

The sale itself received mixed reviews. The press was as eager as the princess to mark a new stage in her life, using the watershed as an excuse to rake over her royal career. The *Sunday Mirror* called the clothes 'elaborate, over-embroidered and frumpy', and claimed that the princess hated the clothes she had been expected to wear to formal dinners. In financial terms, however, the results of the sale were remarkable: it raised more than £2 million. The star item proved to be Edelstein's ink-blue velvet off-the-shoulder dress, which Diana had worn at the White House reception: it sold for a remarkable £133,835.

THE AUCTION WAS THE END of a period of Diana's fashion life; of that there can be little doubt. But it was also the start of a phase, the possible outcome of which must remain a matter of conjecture. Of the designers represented in the sale, only Walker and Azagury were still regular collaborators. Edelstein had retired from fashion to paint in Spain. The others had failed to keep up with the princess's evolving sense of style. As for Diana's other designers, Versace was dead and his sister Donatella had not had time to develop a sure individual touch. Galliano at Dior had been tried and largely rejected. Valentino had supplied dresses for Diana but had angered her over the incident with the premature press release.

Who would have dressed the princess from then on? Roland Klein believes that there would not have been many designers: 'I have a feeling that she was totally aware of what was going on, what was fashionable, what was in and out … but by then she had developed her own style, and eventually she probably would have stuck with a very few people'. Who might they have been? Diana loved Karl Lagerfeld's work for Chanel, and was an eager patron of London designers such as Amanda Wakeley and Rifat Ozbek. Catherine Walker notes in her autobiography that she already sensed it was time for another change in the princess's clothing: 'I anticipated that she would move on to wear more mid-Atlantic clothes'.

Perhaps a sign had come on the princess's visit to Angola with the Red Cross – and a BBC film crew – to publicize the campaign against land mines. Wearing khaki Armani slacks, a plain white shirt with the badge of the Red Cross stitched above the breast pocket and JP Tod's moccasins, Diana posed with the victims of land mines and even walked through a minefield – a literal one this time rather than the figurative ones she was used to. Diana had reduced fashion almost to the point of nonexistence by deliberating selecting the most basic items in her wardrobe. But the anonymity of the clothes did not reduce the effectiveness of the message: the simple symbol of the badge, the armoured vest and glass visor that she wore provided some of the most memorable images of Diana's entire life.

Such simplicity would be less effective back at home, however, where Diana knew that successful working of the crowds depended on creating the image that people wanted to see. Here, she had to dress for attention, as she always had. There is little doubt that Walker and Azagury would have continued to provide the backbone of her working wardrobe. Even after the sale, the clothes they made for her represented not so much a clean break from the past as a gradual evolution that had been going on for a year or more. Walker, for one, looked forward to the next stage, saying: 'I felt thrilled that Diana could at last control her own image. The real person had finally become strong enough to supersede the image'.

Azagury designed the last formal dress that Diana wore in public. He made her a gift of the full-length gown in sequined and beaded black chantilly lace for her thirty-sixth birthday, and that same night she changed her wardrobe plans to wear it to a dinner celebrating the centenary of the Tate Gallery in

BRITISH
RED CROSS
THE
HALO
TRUST

London. It was one of Azagury's favourite dresses for the princess. Soon afterward, Diana sent a driver around to Azagury's boutique with a present – a picture frame holding signed photographs of Diana wearing three of her favourite Azagury outfits, including the birthday dress.

The dress that Diana originally intended to wear to the Tate was another by Azagury, in black silk georgette glittering with thousands of bugle beads. Azagury and Diana had planned it to be 'the most sexy creation Diana had ever worn in public, with a split up the thigh and plunging cleavage which announced her new-found joy at being a woman'.

The princess told the designer that she now proposed to wear it for a film premiere in October, but fate intervened and the dress remained unworn. Diana died on 31 August 1997, after a high-speed car crash in Paris, where she and her new partner, Dodi Al-Fayed, son of the Harrods' owner Mohamed Al-Fayed, were spending a weekend.

Millions of people around the world struggled to come to terms with their sorrow at Diana's death. For profound psychological reasons that reflect how successfully the princess had achieved her ambition to take a place in people's hearts, public grief grew to border on hysteria. Loss is always more difficult to bear when it is sudden, and even more so with a woman of Diana's beauty and youth who had two young children. Millions of women had followed her long struggle for independence, when she had recovered from the misery of her childhood, her eating disorders and her troubled marriage to emerge apparently triumphant. She had shaped her body in the way she wanted it, defied the Establishment, and shown time and time again that she was her own woman. Millions of women shared that journey from the steps of St Paul's Cathedral on the morning of the royal wedding, as the princess tried to find her way back to the fairytale neverland in which her heart told her she should be living. At a time of such tantalizing new beginnings, the realization that Diana's fairytale would have no happy ending magnified the distress. For people of all ages, classes and ethnic origins, Diana had become an inspirational example of what they could achieve and how they could find themselves, even if they were not graced with her wealth and her time.

For Diana's designers, the shock of her death was made worse by the physical traces they still had of her presence. Azagury was left with his last dress, which the princess would never be seen wearing by anyone but him, as

she laughingly catwalked around his studio. Jimmy Choo was due to deliver a pair of beige ballerina flats to Diana the day after she was due home. Catherine Walker had been commissioned for a navy pinstriped jacket and a burnt-red cocktail dress only five days before Diana's death.

Walker's final, fitting commission, however, came from Paul Burrell, Diana's butler, who played a vital role in the funeral preparations. He asked the designer to create a dress for the princess to be buried in. (The body had temporarily been clothed in a black cocktail dress belonging to the wife of the British ambassador in Paris.) Neither designer nor butler has ever discussed the garment, although there is every reason to suppose that it was black. All that Catherine Walker has said is that she set out to make a dress that 'is one she most probably would have bought and would have loved'.

DIANA ONCE ASKED MILLINER PHILIP SOMERVILLE a question that took on a deep pathos after her death: 'If anything happens to me, do you think that people will see me as another Jackie Kennedy?' The answer, it is now clear, is no – and yet perhaps also yes. Jackie Kennedy's sense of style was so unfaltering, so inextricably linked with her personality, that it is impossible to think of her without that Jackie O style. Diana was different: at the time of her death, she was still maturing as a fashionable dresser, having moved on after her divorce to try new designers and new outfits. Some of the new clothes – those of Versace, in particular – seemed as if they might become her signature pieces, but the tragic deaths of both Versace and the princess ended that possibility. So no, Diana was no Jackie Kennedy. And yet, for years, she had been the undoubted fashion leader of the world, the cynosure of glamour in everyone's eyes. And so, in a way, Diana *was* another Jackie, a woman whose appearance made her known and adored around the world. According to the editor of the influential US magazine *Ladies Home Journal*, 'without a doubt she is the greatest media personality of the decade. One comes along every ten years – Jackie, Liz Taylor and now Diana'.

But, for all her global profile, it was in London that the princess's loss was felt most sharply and where her legacy was most thoroughly examined. Victor Edelstein, a designer with a greater grasp of history than most in the fashion world, perceptively compares Diana to Eva Peron, wife of the Argentine dictator: 'They are the two women in this century who had this incredible rapport with the people'. Bruce Oldfield observes: 'She was shaping up to be a world figure in fashion before her death ... She had the power of celebrity without trying'. And for Murray Arbeid, 'She was a very kind and understanding woman. She was beautiful, she had a smashing figure, she was a princess'.

Diana's death left a chasm not just in British fashion but in world fashion. For all her late-flowering desire to be known for her good works rather than her appearance, she had become without question not only the most recognizable figure on the planet after her mother-in-law, but also the most fashionable. American fashion designer Donna Karan, who had not even made formal clothes for the princess, said after her death: 'She was a symbol of what one meant when one spoke of icons ... She was a mentor to women and she set standards'.

From now on,

**I am going to**

**and be**

I no longer

to live someone

of what and

**own myself**
**true to myself.**

want
else's idea
who I should be.

DIANA, PRINCESS OF WALES

## AUTHOR'S ACKNOWLEDGEMENTS

I interviewed many people during the research for this book, the majority of whom preferred to remain anonymous and to keep their contributions off the record. I would particularly like to thank my researchers, Helen Forster, Anita Dalal and Sarah Halliwell. Above all, I am grateful to the designers and others who worked with the Princess of Wales on her appearance for sharing their memories.

## BIBLIOGRAPHY

Burrell, Paul. *A Royal Duty*, Putnam, New York, 2003.

— *The Way We Were: Remembering Diana*. HarperCollins, London, 2006.

Clayton, Tim, and Phil Craig. *Diana: Story of a Princess*, Hodder & Stoughton, London, 2001.

Clehane, Diane. *Diana: The Secrets of her Style*, GT Publishing Corporation, New York, 1998.

Ebbetts, Lesley. *The Royal Style Wars*, Sidgwick & Jackson, London, 1988.

Emanuel, David and Elizabeth. *A Dress for Diana*, Pavilion, London, 2006.

Gauntlett, Alison. *Diana: The Unseen Archives*, Paragon, Bath, 2003.

Graham, Tim. *Diana, Princess of Wales: A Tribute*, Weidenfeld & Nicolson, London, 1997.

Graham, Tim, and Tamsin Blanchard. *Dressing Diana*, Weidenfeld & Nicolson, London, 1998.

Howell, Georgina, *Diana: Her Life in Fashion*, Pavilion, London, 1998.

James, Sue. *The Princess of Wales Fashion Handbook*, Orbis, London, 1984.

Jephson, Patrick. *Portraits of a Princess: Travel with Diana*, Sidgwick and Jackson, London, 2004.

— *Shadows of a Princess: Diana, Princess of Wales, 1987–1996*, Harper Collins, London, 2001.

Mansel, Philip. *Dressed to Rule: Royal and Court Costume from Louis XIV to Elizabeth II*, Yale University Press, New Haven and London, 2005.

McDowell, Colin. *A Hundred Years of Royal Style*, Muller Blond & White, London, 1985

Modlinger, Jackie. *Diana, Queen of Style*, Courage Books, Philadelphia, 1998.

Morton, Andrew. *Diana: Her True Story – In Her Own Words*, Michael O'Mara, London, 1992.

Oldfield, Bruce. *Rootless*, Hutchinson, London, 2004.

Shaw, Martina. *Princess, Leader of Fashion*, Colour Library Books, Godalming, 1983.

Simmons, Simone. *Diana: The Last Word*, Orion, London, 2005.

Tilberis, Liz. *No Time to Die*, Weidenfeld & Nicolson, London, 1998.

Walker, Catherine. *Catherine Walker: An Autobiography by the Private Couturier to Diana, Princess of Wales*, Harper Collins, London, 1998.

*Dresses from the Collection of Diana, Princess of Wales*, Christie's, New York, 1997.

2–3 Princess at peace: a relaxed Diana in a Victor Edelstein dress, photographed by Mario Testino in 1997. © Mario Testino.

4 Diana strikes a princess-like pose in a formal portrait by Snowdon. © Snowdon/Camera Press London.

6 Diana visits the West London Mission in Hinde Street in September 1993. © George Grimes/courtesy National Portrait Gallery, London.

11 The dress that knocked Prince Charles off the front pages: Diana strides out in Christina Stambolian at the Serpentine Gallery, London, on 29 June 1994. © Camera Press London/Diana Memorial Fund.

12 Diana created a storm on her first official engagement with Prince Charles in March 1981 when she nearly fell out of her Emanuel gown. She soon learned to get out of a car more discreetly, and to wear higher necklines. © Alpha Press.

15 Later that evening, the royal couple prepare to leave: Charles reportedly told Diana that women should wear black only when in mourning. © Gettyimages/Central Press.

16 A 1995 portrait by Gemma Levine of Diana in a sailor-suit outfit. © Gemma Levine/Camera Press London.

21 Diana wears her favourite yellow dungarees at a polo match with her friend Sarah Ferguson in 1981. © Tim Graham.

24–5 The princess-to-be smothered by the billowing veil of the Emanuels' wedding dress on the steps of St Paul's on 29 July 1981. The fairytale was already threatening to overwhelm the girl from the shires. © Corbis/Bettmann.

27 Diana as a toddler in her pram. © Alpha Press.

28 Diana plays croquet on holiday at Itchenor in West Sussex in 1970, aged nine. © Gettyimages/Central Press.

31 Diana leaves the Ritz Hotel after celebrating Princess Margaret's fiftieth birthday with the royal family in November 1980, before she even owned an evening coat to cover her ball gown. © Camera Press London/Diana Memorial Fund.

32 Chelsea girl: Diana photographed out-and-about as rumours spread of her engagement to the prince. Polo necks did not flatter her and they were soon virtually dropped from the royal wardrobe. © Popperfoto.

35 Country uniform: trousers by Margaret Howell, green wellies, big socks and a colourful jumper from Inca, London's leading shop for Peruvian textiles, as Diana relaxes with her fiancé on her first trip to Balmoral. © Anwar Hussein.

37 City uniform: Diana gets into her car outside Colherne Court in December 1980. © Camera Press London/Diana Memorial Fund.

38 An official portrait by Snowdon, taken in 1982. Diana felt an affinity with the photographer, who had been, like her, a commoner admitted to what she called 'the Firm'. © Snowdon/*Vogue*/Camera Press London.

41 Diana's fashion naivety was never quite as cruelly exposed as in this notorious shot of the nursery teacher in her Laura Ashley heart-patterned dress. © Rex Features.

42 The portrait taken by Snowdon for *Vogue* appeared fortuitously on the day that the engagement was announced. The chiffon blouse first attracted Diana to the Emanuels, and eventually led to their commission for the wedding dress. © Snowdon/*Vogue*/Camera Press London.

45 Once the engagement was announced, Diana made a conscious effort to dress in a smarter, more grown-up way. © Camera Press London/Diana Memorial Fund.

47 The official engagement dress was an off-the-peg outfit from Harrods with a fussy bow around the neck, worn with flat shoes; Diana's rationale for choosing the rather unflattering garment was that the blue matched her sapphire engagement ring. © Tim Graham.

49 Diana at a 1983 banquet in Auckland, wearing a dress by Gina Fratelli, complete with tiara and the chartreuse yellow family order of Elizabeth II. © Anwar Hussein.

50 Diana wears Jasper Conran for a polo match. The clean, simple lines of the white mohair cardigan went against the grain for the young princess, who still associated sophistication with complexity. © Tim Graham.

53 The wedding dress crumpled in the coach on the way to St Paul's, and never flattened out, even though the designers were on hand to help iron out any problems. © Anwar Hussein.

54 Diana chats to her bridesmaids while waiting with her new mother-in-law to appear on the balcony at Buckingham Palace. The Queen's conservative blue outfit was what passed for royal dressing before Diana stole the limelight. © Patrick Lichfield/Camera Press London.

57 The princess wears Victor Edelstein and the Spencer family tiara to the opera at La Scala, Milan, in 1985. She wore the same dress to a concert by Barry Manilow, to rather more appreciation than it received from Milan's fashion arbiters. © Anwar Hussein.

60 A Roland Klein sketch for an off-the-shoulder ball gown from 1981. Klein's couture is all based on cut, a somewhat old-fashioned virtue he learned from working with Christian Dior and Karl Lagerfeld. © Roland Klein.

64–5 Illustrations © Penny Dann.

67 A formal portrait taken by Snowdon in summer 1981 shows Diana as a fairytale princess, and yet also manages to suggest a certain impatience with the formal demands of the royal role. © Snowdon/Camera Press London.

68 Jan Vanvelden's puritan collars were one of the princess's early trademark looks. Here she plays with Prince William during a trip to New Zealand. © Tim Graham.

71 A Jacques Azagury sketch for a red silk georgette column dress worn by Diana to the Red Cross Ball gala dinner in Washington, DC, in June 1997. © Jacques Azagury.

72 Diana at a polo match in Jan Vanvelden's full-sleeved blouse in a black and white print by celebrated textile designer Zika Ascher. © Tim Graham.

75 Relaxed as she sails off on the royal yacht *Britannia* to her honeymoon and a new life, Diana wears a casual white silk flaconné floral dress by Donald Campbell. © Rex Features.

77 The look that drove Middle England mad: the princess in Brecon in 1981 in a Jaeger suit, 'Lady Di' hat courtesy of John Boyd, hair by Kevin Shanley. © Tim Graham.

78 An early trip to Australia, and the princess is still finding her fashion feet. The veil is a little too fussy, the floral print a little too busy and mumsy – the smile at least is open and confident. © Tim Graham.

81 The Bellville Sassoon design for the 1981 Gonzaga dress that convinced children everywhere that Diana really was something out of a fairytale. © Bellville Sassoon.
82 Pregnant with William, Diana wears the Gonzaga dress to the Victoria and Albert Museum exhibition dedicated to the Renaissance rulers of Mantua – few Renaissance courts rivalled the intrigues of Buckingham Palace over the following decade. © Tim Graham.
85 The U.S. press could not fail to notice Diana, but were perhaps more ready than their British counterparts to consider the economics of the princess's role. © Anwar Hussein/*Time Life*.
88–9 Victor Edelstein designed a dress for Diana to wear to Ascot in 1986, a year in which polka dots were a firm favourite with the princess, if not with her sister-in-law Anne. © Tim Graham.
91 Any trip to Italy was a particular challenge for a princess whose status as a fashion leader made her wardrobe the object of rigorous scrutiny from the fashionistas. This 1985 effort in brown was not one of her most successful responses. © Anwar Hussein.
94–5 At the Cannes Film Festival in 1987, Diana's pale silk chiffon gown by Catherine Walker makes her the centre of attention amid a sea of dark suits. © Rex Features/Steve Wood.
96 When in Scotland… north of the border, Diana was always ready – perhaps a little too ready – to demonstrate her affection by turning to tartan. This Caroline Charles dress and John Boyd beret were worn to the Braemar Games. © Anwar Hussein.
99 Diana's travelling wardrobes and other luggage on the tarmac at Melbourne airport during a tour of Australia. The princess never travelled light. © Tim Graham.
101 Diana's much-anticipated going-away dress for her honeymoon was a pale apricot suit by Bellville Sassoon with a matching hat by John Boyd. © Anwar Hussein.
102 Roland Klein's sketch for one of Diana's favourite garments: a white sweater with a trompe l'oeil scarf knitted into it. © Roland Klein.
106–7 Illustrations © Penny Dann.
109 Diana wears Hachi, with intricate embroidered vermicelli of translucent gold glass beads and crystals, for the premiere of the Bond movie *Octopussy* in 1983. © Anwar Hussein.
110 Snowdon's portrait of Diana with Prince Harry in 1984 gives the princess something of the quality of a Fifties movie star. © Snowdon/Camera Press London.
113 David Sassoon dressed Diana for the opening of the Barbican Arts Centre in 1982 – and showed how glamour and maternity wear were not necessarily mutually exclusive. © Tim Graham.
115 Diana's Edelstein dress swirls as she captivates the Reagans – and irritates her husband – dancing with John Travolta at the White House. © Rex Features.
116 A return to dungarees: Terence Donovan's portrait captures Diana's simple, practical side as she turns up for a photo shoot. © Terence Donovan Archive/Camera Press London.
119 Terence Donovan took this 1990 picture of the princess in Catherine Walker's flamboyant 'Elvis' dress. The origin of the name is clear. © Terence Donovan Archive/Camera Press London.
121 The off-duty princess in pink gingham trousers with Prince William in 1986. © Tim Graham.
122 John Boyd changed his shapes as the 1980s went on, creating hats with larger brims and artificial feathers. © Anwar Hussein.
125 Graham Smith's witty sailor's hat and Catherine Walker's striped suit fit well with Diana's binoculars in this photograph on board ship at La Spezia, Italy, in 1985. © Anwar Hussein.
126 Bruce Oldfield's sketch for a silver lamé dress. © Bruce Oldfield.
129 Dynasty Di: Oldfield's silver lamé and big shoulders on a trip to Australia in 1985. © Anwar Hussein.
130 The pagoda hat by Philip Somerville was worn in a number of countries in East and Southeast Asia. © Anwar Hussein.
133 Diana wears houndstooth check on a visit to Germany in 1987. The pattern was a recurring feature in her daywear wardrobe. © Anwar Hussein.
134 The Veronica Lake hairstyle Diana adopted after the birth of Prince Harry was a little too much of a departure for a woman whom the public largely wanted to look the same at all times. © Rex Features/Nils Jorgensen.
137 It's hard to look glamorous on the ski slopes, as Diana and Sarah Ferguson showed at Klosters in Switzerland in 1987. © Tim Graham.
138 Remembrance chic: Diana in Washington DC in November 1985 pins her poppy to a Catherine Walker suit, which is complemented by a Freddie Fox hat. © Anwar Hussein.
141, 142 Roland Klein's sketch and the dress he created for Ascot in 1985 was a witty play on the black and white pinstripes of the business suit. Diana emphasized the look by carrying a businessman's umbrella. 141 © Roland Klein; 142 © Tim Graham.
146–7 Illustrations © Penny Dann.
149 Diana, wearing Catherine Walker, faces the media at the Taj Mahal in a photocall carefully managed to present the princess as a symbol of forlorn love. © Anwar Hussein.
151 The rising sun from the Japanese flag dominates an outfit for a trip in 1986. © Tim Graham.
152 Catherine Walker designed a suit for a trip to Egypt that was modest enough to follow Islamic dress codes and light and practical for the heat – and a suitable sandy tone to complement the pyramids in the inevitable photographs. © Anwar Hussein.
155 Sketch and fabric swatch by Bellville Sassoon. © Bellville Sassoon.
158–9 Diana chose her 'caring' dress by Bellville Sassoon because she thought the colours reminded people of sweeties. Here she wears it to a children's hostel in São Paolo, Brazil. © Tim Graham.
160 As high as the hemline could go: Diana gets off a motor launch in Venice in 1995 in a Jacques Azagury dress. © Tim Graham.
163 Ready for the boardroom: Diana's face is as determined as her suit is businesslike as she cruises a Venice canal. © Tim Graham.
165 Catherine Walker's 1995 dress takes full advantage of Diana's décolletage and her well-defined upper arms. © Tim Graham.

166 Even in army fatigues, Diana brings a touch of glamour to the act of climbing into a tank. The outfit was made especially for her. © Camera Press London/Diana Memorial Fund.
169 Diana wears Tomasz Starzewski's trademark horizontally pleated dress; the princess's patronage helped Starzewski sell some 400 of the same style, including one to Sarah Ferguson. © Rex Features/News Group.
170 A long tunic shirt and lightweight pyjama trousers were Catherine Walker's answer to the problem of Islamic modesty – and sitting on low cushions – during a tour to the Gulf States in 1989. © Rex Features/David Levenson.
173 Diana dazzles in the Victor Edelstein dress that was the highlight of her trip to Paris in 1988. © Tim Graham.
174 Catherine Walker researched the customs of the Catholic church for this veil worn by Diana on a trip to the Vatican in 1985, when prince and princess had an audience with the pope. © Tim Graham.
177 The night the princess got soaked at an open-air Pavarotti concert in Hyde Park. Diana wears a Paul Costelloe jacket, royal jewellery and an excited smile. © Tim Graham.
178 Though known as one of fashion's wild boys, Gianni Versace could produce suits that were almost conservative in their cut – if not in their colour. The Lady Dior handbag, given to Diana by the French First Lady, Bernadette Chirac, was hugely popular. © Tim Graham.
181 A Starzewski dress and a Philip Somerville hat for VJ Day celebrations in 1995. © Tim Graham.
184–5 Illustrations © Penny Dann.
187 Catherine Walker showed that she could cut a mean business suit with this pink outfit from 1997. © Tim Graham.
188 Diana on her way to the gym: she was probably the best-known exerciser in the country. © Alpha Press.
191 This dress by Valentino was worn by Diana a couple of times in 1992. © Valentino.
192 A satin and lace outfit for a theatre trip echoes the shape of the famous Edelstein dress worn in Paris in 1988, but is less successful in its shape around the waist. © Tim Graham.
195 Typically strong patterns from Moschino in a jacket that owes much to Coco Chanel. © Tim Graham.
196 In December 1995, Diana collected a Humanitarian Award in New York, and wore a Versace dress with a cross back and a daring new décolletage. © Tim Graham.
199 More Versace at a gala dinner in Chicago, worn with matching Jimmy Choo shoes. Diana had become a truly international fashion figure, as at home in great American and European cities as she was in London. © Tim Graham.
202–3 Possibly the second most famous pink pillbox hat in fashion history. Versace's suit was another homage to Jackie Kennedy, one of Diana's fashion heroines. © Tim Graham.
205 Great photographers tell stories: Snowdon put Diana next to a horse, which she disliked, to emphasize the tension in the royal marriage in 1991. © Snowdon/Camera Press London.
207 A single strand of pearls and a softly tailored Versace suit – the older Diana became far more comfortable in herself and no longer fussed up her clothes in an effort to protect herself. © Camera Press London/Washington Photos.
208 Diana wears Catherine Walker's tribute to Hollywood glamour – a long black dress with a halter neck edged in bugle beads. © Rex Features/News Group.
211 A working wardrobe for an international campaigner: Diana wears a sleeveless chambray shirt, khakis and loafers as she shares a smile with mine victim Sandra Thijka on a visit to Angola in January 1997. © Tim Graham.
212 Diana gained the confidence to trust that less is more. Here, she is seen in a deceptively simple Versace dress for a fund-raising Pavarotti concert in Italy. © Tim Graham.
215 On holiday on the Caribbean island of Necker in 1990, Diana wore a leopard-print swimsuit and a matching skirt to meet the press, starting a craze for leopard-print swimwear. © Tim Graham.
216 Sketch for a 1993 evening gown by Bellville Sassoon. © Bellville Sassoon.
219 Diana wears a fuchsia pink silk gown by Victor Edelstein. The off-the-shoulder cowl is inspired by the fashions of the Thirties. © Tim Graham.
220 Wearing the notorious 'nightdress' by Galliano at Dior, Diana arrives with friend Liz Tilberis at the Costume Institute Ball in New York in December 1996. The outstanding British designer of his generation completely misunderstood the demands of dressing the princess. © Tim Graham.
223 A classic pale blue bouclé suit by Chanel, worn by Diana to the British Lung Foundation in London. She carries a bunch of Princess of Wales roses, named in her honour. © Tim Graham.
224 Diana arrives at the London preview of the Christie's auction of her dresses in a simple but heavily embroidered Catherine Walker shift that echoed the opulence of royal dressing from the Tudor age, but also emphasized the shoulders, upper arms and chest of Diana's very modern figure. © Tim Graham.
227 The clothes are no longer the story: a Ralph Lauren shirt and khakis take second place to the Halo Trust body armour on a visit to mine-clearing operations in Angola. Diana had come a long way from her tailored army fatigues (see page 166). © Tim Graham.
229 Jacques Azagury was one of the designers who understood Diana best in the last months of her life. The designer gave her this dress for her thirty-sixth birthday and she wore it at a gala dinner to celebrate the centenary of the Tate Gallery. © Tim Graham.
230 Like her other designers, Roland Klein took advantage of the greater freedom Diana had following her separation to put her in simpler dresses that emphasized her long legs and broad shoulders. This was the last dress he designed for her. © Roland Klein.
233 By the end of her life, Diana, seen here at Buenos Aires airport, had become one of the elite international group of wealthy women who can afford to spend huge amounts of money on clothes that do not advertise their value. © Tim Graham.
236 Taking pleasure in herself for a moment, the princess makes a surprise appearance on stage at the Royal Opera House in 1986 to dance with Wayne Sleep. © Rex Features/Helen Wilson.